6/06

# UNRAVELLING ENIGMA

# UNRAVELLING ENIGMA

## Winning the Code War at Station X

by

## MAURICE FREEDMAN

LEO COOPER

First published in Great Britain in 2000 by
LEO COOPER
an imprint of
Pen & Sword Books Ltd
47 Church Street
Barnsley
South Yorkshire
S70 2AS

A catalogue record for this book is
available from the British Library

ISBN 0 85052 747 3

Typeset in 10.5/12.5 Sabon
by Phoenix Typesetting, Ilkley, West Yorkshire.

Printed in Great Britain by
Redwood Books Ltd, Trowbridge, Wilts.

To
Audrey

# CONTENTS

# ACKNOWLEDGEMENTS

My thanks are due, in the first instance, to Nora Millward, without whose generous loan of several volumes of the Official History, *British Intelligence in the Second World War*, I might not have started. Ralph Parker, one of the stalwarts of Hut Six, was kind enough to read the script at an early stage, and generously gave me a splendid picture of Hut Six staff celebrating Victory in Europe Day, 8 May 1945. Peter Calvocoressi gave friendly encouragement. Peter Coast cast a mathematical eye over some of the more technical passages. I owe a good deal to my lecture audiences, some of whom were personally involved in code-breaking or allied activities and whose searching questions, as well as helpful suggestions, have helped to keep me on the right track.

The following authors and publishers have given permission to quote extracts from their publications:

Antony Beevor, *Crete – The Battle and the Resistance* (John Murray (Publishers) Ltd, 1993).
Ralph Bennett, *Ultra in the West: The Normandy Campaign of 1944–45* (Hutchinson, 1979).
Ralph Bennett, *Ultra and Mediterranean Strategy, 1941–45* (Hamish Hamilton, 1989).
Peter Calvocoressi, *Top Secret Ultra* (Cassell, 1980).
F.H. Hinsley et al., *British Intelligence in the Second World War*, Official History. Crown Copyright is reproduced with the

permission of the Controller of Her Majesty's Stationery Office.

F.H. Hinsley and Alan Stripp (eds), *Codebreakers: The Inside Story of Bletchley Park* (1993). Reprinted by permission of Oxford University Press.

Andrew Hodges, *Alan Turing: The Enigma* (Vintage, 1992).

David Kahn, *Seizing the Enigma* (Souvenir Press, 1992).

Christopher Morris, *Navy Ultra's Poor Relations,* from Intelligence and National Security, Vol. 1, No. 1 (1986) (Frank Cass & Co. Ltd).

*The Oxford Companion to the Second World War* (1995). Reprinted by permission of Oxford University Press.

Gordon Welchman, *The Hut Six Story* (Baldwin, 1997).

Picture credits: pictures 1–7, Bletchley Park Trust/Science and Society Picture Library.

Jacket Illustration, Bletchley Park Trust/Science and Society Picture Library.

The King hath note of all that they intend,
By interception which they dream not of.

*Henry V* (Act II, Scene II)

# INTRODUCTION

If the astonishing code-breaking carried out at Bletchley Park during the Second World War was truly 'Britain's greatest twentieth-century achievement', and helped to shorten the War, it deserves better treatment in print and in the media than it has so far received.

To those who have been confused, indeed perplexed, by what they have already read or seen of code-breaking, as well as those coming new to this topic, I offer a straightforward, readable account, where the reader may follow the story without being discouraged by mathematics and technology. I have tried to keep necessary explanations as clear as possible, and avoid the jargon which so often plagues this subject. I have also sketched in some of the wartime background against which these events took place, and have looked at the role played by Ultra intelligence (the secret information obtained by code- and cipher-breaking) in some of the great land battles of the War, as well as examining its part in the Battle of the Atlantic.

British code- and cipher-breaking attained a huge success in the Second World War, when, for the first time in history, one side was consistently listening, on a very large scale, to the secret military intelligence of the other.

The essence of that achievement was the sheer scale of the operation. Whereas the Poles had determinedly broken the German Enigma ciphering system from 1933–8, although without obtaining much information, the British created, out of a chaotic intelligence situation, one big organization capable of deciphering and processing thousands of secret enemy signals every day, turning them into valuable information, often vital for the conduct of the War. Complex and difficult as these processes undoubtedly were, they were accomplished with assembly-line precision and in industrial production quantities.

The British learned to know their enemy as well, and sometimes better, than he knew himself. It was said that if, in 1944, you wanted to find three people who knew more about the German Air Force than anyone else, they would be found, not in Germany, but at Bletchley Park!

For a country which, at Dunkirk, had suffered a most humiliating retreat, and seemed in 1940 almost certain to lose the War, possession of this 'secret weapon' proved, by 1944, when the Allied invasion of Europe took place, to be of supreme value.

The story of code- and cipher-breaking and the Ultra top secret intelligence it produced, has been bedevilled by two factors. First, Bletchley Park, in wartime, operated a very stringent 'need to know' rule – 'if it's not your job, don't ask' – and a tight division of labour, so that perhaps fifty or sixty out of 7,000 people had an overall, although not a detailed, picture of the work.

Then there was a time-lag of some thirty-three years before the secrecy restrictions were lifted – and then not completely – in 1978, and officially, at least, no private written records of this secret wartime activity should have been kept.

The combined effect of the 'need to know' – what one Bletchley veteran called, 'the tunnel vision from which we all suffer' – and the fading memories, became evident when the ban was lifted in 1978. Books and articles appeared, some of which were wide of the mark, spreading misinformation and confusion, especially as information emerged in piecemeal fashion. Most aspects of the Second World War have a generally agreed history, but owing to the long official silence, the code-breaking story was far from clear. Then the authorized *History of British Intelligence in the Second World War* began to appear (five vols; 1979–90) and things started to improve, but by then a good deal of damage had been done. A lot of misinformation still persists; indeed, it is difficult to read a newspaper article, a reference book or an obituary notice without being aware of the errors still in circulation. Nor was the television series about Bletchley Park of much help, leaving many of its viewers more confused than enlightened. Leaving aside its inaccuracies, what I found particularly irksome was the absence of any recognition of Gordon Welchman, without whom Bletchley Park, as we know it, would not have existed. Very early in the War Welchman saw that it was not a matter of breaking a few secret enemy codes, but in order to make a real impact on the outcome of the War Bletchley would have to decode or decipher hundreds and probably thousands, of messages every single day. Accordingly, he planned a large, round-the-clock, code-breaking organization, and persuaded his bosses to take immediate action. Had they not done so they would not have survived.

Wolshman's second great contribution was to develop Turing's experimental 'Bombe' – a machine to help in large-scale deciphering – by a modification so dramatic that it could then cope with increased numbers and with a greatly reduced margin of error, so that, in the words of Turing's biographer, 'the Bombe would enjoy an almost uncanny elegance and power'. This quite serious omission may be no more than another example of the now common media attitude, 'why let the facts spoil a good story?'

An early source of misinformation had been Group Captain Winterbotham, a senior wartime Secret Service officer, who had obtained permission to publish as early as 1974, and whose book, *The Ultra Secret*, first in the field and widely read, contained a variety of misleading and even sensational statements. The story, which I encountered several times when lecturing on 'Ultra' subjects, that Churchill allowed Coventry to be bombed in 1940 because defending it would have revealed to the enemy that their messages were being deciphered, comes from this book, and is without foundation. Typical of Winterbotham's attitude is his whimsical, and quite unforgivable, description of the Bletchley Park 'Bombe' as being, 'like some Eastern Goddess who was destined to become the oracle of Bletchley'. As he should have known, this 'oracle' only gave the correct answer when fed with very accurate estimates of part of what the original – but still enciphered – enemy message contained! This was a mind-boggling, nerve-racking task to try the skill, brains and patience of Bletchley's saints and geniuses, the agony being compounded by having to start afresh each day, as the enemy changed his ciphering arrangements at midnight! I am reminded of the American music devotee who gushed, 'Oh, Mr Heifetz, your violin sounds so wonderful!' 'Oh,' said Heifetz, looking at the instrument in his hands, 'I don't hear anything!'

# Terminology

I have used the term code-making to describe preparing a communication between two parties which is to be kept secret, and code-breaking when an unauthorized third party decodes or 'breaks' the secret code.

In this book we are concerned mainly with ciphers in which individual letters are disguised, and here I have preferred encipher and decipher, rather than encrypt and decrypt (or worse, encryption and decryption), now in common use, but not current during the War, and which come from the US. Similarly, I have avoided cryptographer for one who prepares a code or cipher, and cryptanalyst for one who breaks codes and ciphers.

During the War the word 'decoding' was in common use, regardless of whether codes or ciphers were broken, the successful results called 'decodes', and this will appear where appropriate.

# 'Speed of attack through speed of communications'

The German military theory of 'blitzkrieg', of lightning war, was designed for an aggressive country that was not rich in resources, and as the First World War had shown, could not survive a prolonged conflict. The aim was to overwhelm its victims with highly mobile armoured divisions, motorized infantry, self-propelled guns, all preceded by squadrons of dive-bombers spreading destruction and terror ahead of the advancing armies, and these methods took first Poland, then Western Europe, by surprise in 1939/40. Combined operations on this scale demand a very high degree of co-ordination, and that, in turn, requires swift and reliable communication. In the 1930s the Germans would hold conferences in which these blitzkrieg tactics were openly proclaimed, the aim being to intimidate their neighbours.

At one of these conferences Sir William Stephenson, a wireless expert, asked how their air force would get ground support so far ahead of the army. The Air Minister, General Erhard Milch, replied,

> The dive-bombers will form a flying artillery directed to work in harmony with ground forces through good wireless communications, you, [i.e. Stephenson] a wireless expert, must appreciate that for the first time in history, this co-ordination of forces is possible. The air force will not require ground support, any more than the armoured divisions will need repair units. Tanks and planes will be disposable. The real secret is speed, speed of attack through speed of communications.[1]

That disposable machines would include disposable crews, would have gone without saying.

Such far-ranging and high-speed warfare would far outstrip telephone and teleprinter communication; only wireless would serve. Wireless, however, especially small, portable, short-wave equipment, could be heard by friend and foe alike. What was needed therefore, was a system of coding which would be easy for the cipher clerks to learn and use, reliable in blitzkrieg conditions, and above all, one that could never be broken by an enemy. Between the wars the great powers were gradually adopting the use of cipher machines and here the Germans were ahead. The military Enigma machine was fully in service by 1930

5

and its operating system was steadily improved up to 1939. Commanders of Panzer divisions, for example, would have a 'command and control' vehicle equipped with both Enigma and wireless from which they might call up air support, control their own units and also keep in touch with their parent headquarters.

## Note

1. Quoted in Welchman, *The Hut Six Story* (Cleobury Mortimer, Baldwin, 1997), p. 20.

# Chapter 1

# 'GENTLEMEN DO NOT READ EACH OTHER'S MAIL'

Modern British code-breaking really begins with the Royal Navy at the time of the First World War. Right at the outset the British gained a very significant advantage. The German cruiser *Magdeburg*, which ran aground off the island of Odensholm at the entrance to the Gulf of Finland in August 1914, was hastily destroyed to prevent it falling into Russian hands, but the Russians recovered the main *Signalbuch der Kaiserlichen Marine* (Codebook of the Imperial Navy, copy No. 151) from the wreck, and handed it over to their British allies who were the principal naval power at the time, Mr Churchill being the First Lord of the Admiralty. By a further stroke of good fortune the British Admiralty had just established the nucleus of a code-breaking section under the then Director of Naval Education, Sir Alfred Ewing, assisted by, among others, instructors in German from the Royal Naval colleges, including Alastair Denniston, later to be the first head of Bletchley Park. They made little progress with this 'great gift' from the Russians, and hopes began to fade when another codebook was recovered, this time from a merchant ship off the coast of Australia.

This was a merchant marine code (*Handelsschiffsverkehrsbuch*) or HVB: including a method to be used to disguise the special four-letter codewords. Thus, letters in a list would replace the letters in the codewords. As we are now talking about letters rather than words, we may call it a cipher, and say that this second layer of protection is called 'superencipherment'. The British soon realized that this letter

7

replacement system, as used in a fairly modest code for merchant ship-ping, was exactly the same as that used for the German Emperor's Navy! Suddenly, the infant code-breaking section had more work than it could manage, and it moved into larger premises in Room 40 of the Admiralty's Old Building in London.

This astonishing piece of German foolishness had enabled the British, as early as November 1914, to read the encoded wireless traffic put out by the whole German Fleet. The sea continued to yield up prizes to the fortunate Royal Navy, including a *Verkehrsbuch*, a five-digit code used by German officers of flag rank, and new editions of codes at later stages in the War, dredged up or recovered by divers, e.g. from U-boats sunk in the fairly shallow waters around the coasts of Britain. The German Imperial Navy however, obstinately refused to believe that their codes were being broken, despite a large body of evidence to the contrary, including the undeniable fact that the movements of their ships were being precisely anticipated by the British. When the fact had to be faced it was put down to spying, or to betrayal, especially by the lower ranks, or indeed anything except code-breaking. One might reasonably imagine that when the Germans themselves were listen-ing, even by accident, to British naval wireless messages, they might conclude that the enemy was doing the same; but they were only interested in the frequency, call signs and range of such transmissions, not what the messages might actually contain! It was not until the middle of 1917 that the Imperial German Naval Signalbook was finally replaced. This incredible refusal to believe in your own code system's vulnerability was mirrored in the Second World War, as we shall see, with astounding consequences for both sides. It is worth mentioning, before we leave this topic, that the rules under which German naval manoeuvres took place did not permit one side to gain an 'unfair' advantage by listening to the radio signals of the other – the Imperial German equivalent of 'not cricket'!

'Intelligence', between the wars, did not have a good image; secret services and their very secret activities were regarded with no small degree of suspicion, not to say distaste, by the armed forces, politicians and the general public. Besides, in the eyes of 'right thinking persons' such activities were hardly respectable. Henry Stimson, on becoming US Secretary of State in the late 1920s, was horrified to discover his department ran a flourishing cipher bureau. 'Gentlemen,' thundered Stimson, 'do not read each other's mail,' and promptly closed it down.

8

As for 'listening-in', as they would have said, to other people's private wireless transmissions, reading other people's telegrams and tapping telephone lines, it was hardly work for gentlemen. Several British ambassadors of the period were known definitely to disapprove of the activities of the Secret Intelligence Service (SIS), 'the secret service', although they must have become very grand, as it had long been thought that 'An ambassador is an honest man sent to lie abroad for the good of his country.'[1]

When in 1919, the British government of the day decided that, as a result of successful decoding during the war just ended, a Government Code and Cypher School (GC&CS) should be created, its work would be the responsibility of the Secret Service. Resulting from the, at times, disastrous lack of co-operation in intelligence matters during the First World War, this was to be an inter-service organization, ostensibly to devise new British codes and ciphers, and, it goes without saying, to study, and if possible break into, the codes and ciphers of others.

The new 'school', the name probably devised by some Foreign Office wag, began with an experienced staff of about twenty-five, mostly ex-Admiralty Room 40,[2] and some army code-breakers from MI 1(b), with one of the Room 40 men, Alastair Denniston, in charge. In 1922 it came under the administrative control of the Foreign Office, which would eventually cause distinguished code-breakers in the Second World War to have their war service recorded as e.g. 'Foreign Office, 1940-45'.

The three service intelligence departments, always jealous, were resentful of the newcomer 'encroaching' on their territory. They envisaged any future wartime situation as one in which all aspects of deciphered signal intelligence ('sigint' in the official parlance) should go straight from GC&CS to their own intelligence branch – i.e. if they had not managed to subvert the new organization altogether and recover code-breaking for themselves!

In many countries there were several code-breaking establishments, usually bitter rivals. Germany had six or seven, only one of which turned out to be efficient, but that one, as we shall see, was very efficient indeed.

## The School

Meanwhile, the new 'School' (from 1926, at 54 Broadway, in Central London – SIS HQ) did fairly well against the diplomatic codes of a number of countries, but service needs were not entirely forgotten, a naval section being formed in 1924, an army section in 1930 and an air section in.1936. In the mid-1930s the School enjoyed some success against the military and naval codes and ciphers of several countries including Italy, whose aggressive invasion of Abyssinia, and intervention in the Spanish Civil War, caused increasing alarm to the British, who sensed danger to their strategic positions at both ends of the Mediterranean. GC&CS realized that the Italians were using machine encipherment and that the machine in use was similar to the commercial version of the Enigma with which they were already familiar. This machine lacked the modifications made by the German military, and Dillwyn Knox and his colleagues at the School, using traditional methods, were able to determine the keys used and successfully deciphered not only Italian traffic but that of Franco's rebel troops.

The high point for GC&CS was 1937 when their list of successes included several 'great powers', but not Germany. When the Germans went over to machine ciphers in 1926,[3] GC&CS seemed to have been permanently discouraged. In those days, of course, Germany was regarded as a defeated power of little consequence, with any threat to the British Empire or influence likely to come from Japan, the US or the Soviet Union. In any case, German military wireless transmissions in the mid-1930s were not easy to pick up in the British Isles, because the main German Army home organization was using medium-wave transmitters with a limited range, and as it later became apparent, used the Enigma machine, in the twenty home military districts, with strict, thoroughgoing procedures and properly trained men, so that, after 1939 the system was rarely broken.

By 1937, when GC&CS got around to considering German naval traffic after a lapse of ten years, they realized that not only were the three armed services using the Enigma but state organizations such as the SD (Nazi Party security), the railways and certain police as well. The Enigma system was still undergoing that process of continuing modification, which, as we shall see, finally defeated the Poles.

## War Clouds

Nevertheless, right up to the outbreak of war in 1939 the small German sub-section of GC&CS Naval Section could not boast a single code-breaker, let alone a mathematician.

By the mid-1930s the European political scene was in ferment with Hitler rearming madly and bullying his neighbours, civil war in Spain with Germany and Italy openly intervening, Abyssinia being invaded, all countries beginning to rearm and the future looking grim. All this served to concentrate a few minds in British intelligence. It began to be realized that information derived from foreign wireless transmissions came from a number of sources which were handled by different bodies but which cried out for co-ordination as they were clearly interdependent. For example, interception of signals was in the hands of the separate armed services and these listening stations needed to be connected, preferably by teleprinter, to the organization doing the deciphering.

Direction-finding, often done by several D/F stations working together, needed to make the results available to a central co-ordinating body who would then know not only what the intercepted messages contained, if deciphered, but where they came from, and if from a military unit or a naval vessel – had it changed its position? Again, the left hand was not allowed to know what the right hand was doing. Then there is the technique known as 'traffic analysis' which, without deciphering a single word, can tell the shrewd and experienced analyst a great deal about the wireless transmission in question by studying the 'externals' of the traffic: call signs, addressees, wireless frequencies, times of transmission (often given in plain language in the preamble), whether such transmitters were organized in groups or networks ('Sternen' – star-shaped groups of transmitting stations) and whether such stations or groups were linked to any military organization. Then, after the intercepted signals had been deciphered, which was GC&CS's basic function, how was such information to be understood? What did the messages actually mean? They were often mere snippets of information which would mean nothing to the uninitiated. A military message might say that unit 'x', perhaps referred to by a code number, was moving from 'y' to 'z', also referred to by code numbers or names or coded map references. Being able to interpret these miscellaneous scraps requires not only knowledgeable and experienced intelligence officers but, just as important, an existing body of knowledge – e.g. about a particular country's armed forces – to which the intelligence officer could refer. This would need to be carefully built up, on paper, as essential background into which the newly acquired scrap could be fitted, and once fitted, make sense. Then, and only then, could the

11

officer function efficiently and let his civil or service masters have a piece of comprehensible and useful information.

## Military intelligence – a contradiction in terms?

In September 1939, the state of war between Great Britain and Germany notwithstanding, GC&CS's position vis-à-vis the service intelligence directorates was one of stalemate. Despite earlier success in intercepting signals from Italy and Japan, both of whom were engaged in military operations, so producing sufficient wireless traffic for deciphering to become possible, no progress was made after 1937 against German or Russian high-grade (i.e. important) signals, and the Japanese success proved short-lived. Even allowing for the fact that these totalitarian states, for security reasons, used land-lines extensively and wireless infrequently, the Official History comments tartly, 'it remains unfortunate that despite the growing effort applied at GC&CS to military work after 1936, so little attention was paid to the German problem.'[4] Neither did GC&CS have much luck with German diplomatic traffic. But the greater tragedy was that even if the 'School' had produced better results with German signal intelligence the armed services were simply not in a position to take advantage of it. The Official History makes the point in restrained official terms, 'The intelligence branches in Whitehall were as yet unpractised in the art of inferring plans and intentions from the evidence of sigint which, if always incontestable, is also always incomplete.'[5] Primarily, this means that the 'wireless picture' will be incomplete as some part of the intelligence will usually go by land-line. It also implies the absence of an existing body of knowledge, as mentioned above, and indeed, of capable and experienced intelligence officers.

A striking illustration of this chaotic intelligence situation occurred when the Germans invaded Norway in April 1940. If the intelligence services had been worth anything, this sea-borne invasion, with Britain in control of the seas, would surely have been foiled or at least rendered extremely costly to the enemy. For this combined operation the Germans used a special Enigma cipher key (the Yellow) which was broken at GC&CS five days after the operation commenced and was read every day thereafter. This gave information the British Chiefs of Staff would have needed and usually within a few hours. (With fewer land-lines the Luftwaffe information must often have been fairly complete.) 'For the enormous volume of the operational decrypts [deciphered messages] it yielded, no less than for the speed at which it was possible to find the daily settings [in order to decipher the messages], the breaking of the Norwegian Enigma came as a complete surprise. And the first consequence was that neither GC&CS nor the Whitehall departments were equipped to handle the decrypts efficiently.' Thus, 'little or no use could be made of it'(!)[6] On the positive side, the information gained in that hectic month was the first hard military intelligence to come the way of the British – enemy organization, equipment, plans – and probably helped to lay the foundation of that great store-house of enemy information, the 'Index', which was to be built up so assiduously at Bletchley Park and was used to startling effect in turning tiny scraps of information into valuable, often vital, military intelligence.

But it drove home a hard lesson, that even the best intelligence is of little operational value if one is not in a position to use it.

In 1938, with war threatening, the intelligence authorities began to realize that Nazi Germany was a threat to peace and stability in Europe, that its forces were using ciphers based on a military version of the Enigma machine, and that any break into that system would require unified action by all concerned. This, together with the factors already mentioned, militated in favour of co-ordinated effort by one body in one place. It caused the inter-departmental sub-committee concerned to recommend that all interception and direction-finding stations be connected to GC&CS and to each other by telephone and teleprinter, and this was put in hand. They further recommended that a section be established at GC&CS to include traffic analysis and D/F. But this was too much for the jealous service departments because, to quote the Official History, 'this would have extended the work of GC&CS beyond the acquisition and provision of information and infringed their [the service departments] individual responsibility for appreciating and evaluating it.'[7] Thereupon, compromise agreements were worked out which just conceded that GC&CS could retain its service sections and therefore continue as an inter-departmental organization in time of war – itself a reversal of some previous decisions. GC&CS ended up worse off when traffic analysis staff were actually removed, although it

13

was obvious that deciphering and traffic analysis were interdependent. Control of listening stations became the joint responsibility of GC&CS and the service departments.

## Notes

1. Sir Henry Wotton, 1568–1639.
2. Strictly, NID25 (Naval Intelligence Division)
3. See Appendix 1, The Codewheel.
4. Hinsley, F.H. et al., *British Intelligence in the Second World War* (The Official History), Vol. 1 (London, HMSO, 1979), p. 54.
5. Ibid. p. 55.
6. Ibid. p. 137.
7. Ibid. p. 24.

# Chapter 2

# THE POLISH ENIGMA

The new Polish state, created by the Versailles Treaty after the First World War, was always vulnerable, flanked as it was by two defeated but still would-be great powers, Germany and the Soviet Union; resentful, watchful and planning revenge. Even in the 1920s, well before Hitler came to power, loud claims were being heard from some quarters in defeated Germany for the return of Danzig, Poland's new and only outlet to the sea, and the linking Polish corridor, which separated East Prussia from the rest of Germany. The new 'democratic' German post-war Weimar government subjected Poland to considerable 'great power' bullying, and if the infant state was too poor to afford modern weapons of defence, it might at least try to discover what its potential enemies were up to. Accordingly, a small Cipher Bureau was set up in 1920, and by 1928 they noticed a change in German wireless transmissions which led them to believe that the Germans had gone over to enciphering their messages by machine. Realizing that the new method meant letters rather than words, roughly ciphers and not codes, they recruited a small team of mathematicians including Marian Rejewski, with the hope of breaking into, and deciphering, the new German system.

General (then Captain) Bertrand, head of the Cipher Bureau of French Intelligence (*Deuxième Bureau*) in the 1930s, tells in his memoirs how he was in touch with a German whose code-name as a French agent was Asche, but whose real name was Hans-Thilo Schmidt, a declassé, sorely in need of money. This man, from his humble, poorly paid, but sensitive position in the German military cipher office, was able to supply Bertrand with several hundred documents about the workings

15

of the Enigma system during the crucial years 1932–8. Bertrand describes several visits to Warsaw when he handed over copies of the stolen documents to Polish Intelligence, such co-operation being in the spirit of the Franco-Polish Treaty. Schmidt decided he could do better with Enigma documents than consign them to the fires of the boiler in the basement. He showed considerable ingenuity in finding the French Intelligence contact man, and thereafter met the people from Paris at a variety of rendezvous including Belgium, Switzerland and on one occasion was treated to the show at the Folies Bergères. With the help of these documents Marian Rejewski was able, towards the end of 1932, to work out the wiring of the codewheels of the German military Enigma machine, and before very long they had simulated versions of the machine made for their own use. With these new machines they hoped to be in the same position as a German army cipher clerk whose Enigma machine had been set up to receive messages. Rejewski's bosses are believed to have encouraged him to try and break the Enigma machine by theoretical means alone, but it did not prove possible. Without the stolen documents (an operating manual and two or three out-of-date key lists), Rejewski would not have been able to make his initial breakthrough, as he later admitted.

A brief description of the machine now follows. The Enigma is essentially a letter-swapping machine whereby a typewriter-style keyboard is connected electrically to a set of lamps each of which lights up a letter of the alphabet. Each time say, the B key on the keyboard is pressed a differently-lettered lamp will light up. For example, if B is pressed three times, the lamps K, Z, J may light up. The designers of the machine would not like, for example, B to light up K more often than any other letter, so they made the electric current from key to lamp take a complicated and constantly changing route through the machine. To do this they used a set of three revolving wheels, the first of which moved one step every time a key was pressed, and also a set of wired plugs which could be inserted into a plugboard in different ways, which complicated the route from key to lamp a great deal more. The wheels and plugs were adjusted by the clerk before enciphering a message according to printed 'setting-up' instructions known as a key. As the lettered lamps lit up a second clerk would write down the message, letter by letter, and usually give it to a wireless operator to send in Morse code. (see Appendix 1). Unravelling the Enigma machine was a truly outstanding achievement for one individual, but breaking the keys and deciphering messages on a daily basis required teamwork, and two other young mathematicians were recruited, Zygalski and Rozycki. The new team discovered a serious flaw in the procedure then used by the Germans for the operation of the machine.

## Probing the enemy's weak point

The printed setting-up instructions contained four operations to be carried out by the clerk: putting the three wheels (which were removable) in the correct order; turning the special alphabet rings, which surrounded the wheels, to the stated positions, and connecting the plugs as instructed. Then for the fourth operation, the wheels were turned to what the instructions called the 'ground setting' (*Grundstellung*); three specified letters, say KRJ. Having so far followed printed instructions, the clerk was then required to choose three letters of his own, entirely at random. If he chose, say, JGL, he would then tap them out on the keyboard, but he would do it twice, JGLJGL, which might be enciphered by the machine as say, MPYKSR. This is called the indicator and becomes the first six letters of the message. He would then turn his wheels to JGL and encipher the message. As the receiving clerk, following the same instructions, will already have had his machine set up to the same ground setting, KRJ, he will be able to decipher the randomly-chosen three-letter indicator – by tapping out MPYKSR he will get JGLJGL – then set his wheels to JGL and be able to decipher the main body of the message. The reason the indicator letters were repeated was to make sure that no letters had become distorted during wireless transmission, the two groups of three seen to be identical. This repeated, or double encipherment of the indicator, however, proved a serious procedural weakness, and was the main route by which the Poles found their way into the system.

To find a key, the Poles searched through all their intercepted messages each day hoping to exploit the fact that the first and fourth of the six-letter indicators were enciphered versions of the same (unknown) letter. In the example given, if JGLJGL became MPYKSR, both M and K would be versions of J as enciphered by the machine. The same applied to the second and fifth, and third and sixth letters.[1] Using both theoretical analysis and mechanical aids, often slow and tedious to use, they managed to deduce the identity and starting positions of the wheels at the point the indicator letters were enciphered. The other settings were then worked out, the Poles' own machine set up accordingly, and the messages deciphered. A brilliant success and as early as 1932.

Rejewski made these discoveries mainly by the use of group theory, a form of higher algebra. Previous attacks on cipher machines had used probability methods. The leading American code-breaker, William F. Friedman, the man who led the successful attack against the Japanese 'Purple' machine in 1940, had first broken Hebern's five-wheel machine using probability methods, in 1924.

The Poles had, moreover, if not defeated, at least by-passed, the plugboard, the German designers' special pride, introduced in 1930, which had made the really big difference between the commercial and the military versions of the machine. The plugboard had increased to billions, the number of states the machine could be in, and the number of possibilities an enemy code-breaker might have to test, i.e. if he lived long enough! The addition of the plugboard had brought the Enigma machine to the 'unbreakable' condition, or so its designers believed. Apart from one design weakness and one glaring oversight, however, it was not so much the machine that let the Germans down, but faulty procedures, human error or indifference, and failure to monitor the system in practice. Aware that their procedures might have loopholes, the Germans continued to make changes right up to 1939, and, as we shall see, a big change from the code-breakers' point of view, in May 1940, just before the invasion of western Europe.

What the designers had failed to appreciate was that the basic reciprocal nature of the machine – if tapping letter G gives S, then tapping letter S would produce G; and that no letter could ever be enciphered to itself (tapping A never gives A) – was not altered by the addition of the plugboard, which, for purposes of practical analysis, could be partly ignored by the code-breakers, who could boil billions down to millions, which, to mathematicians, may be manageable numbers.

## Sudden changes – rapid responses

The Poles had succeeded because they were quick to spot and exploit a serious procedural weakness – the double encipherment of the three-letter indicator – and because they had, in Marian Rejewski, an outstanding mathematician and code-breaker. Moreover, they

18

remained sufficiently flexible and resourceful to be able to respond to German changes.

Germany's huge rearmament programme, begun in 1935, was reflected in the signal intelligence situation, with wireless gradually coming more into use as new military units were formed and needed practice. The German experts of the *Chiffrierstelle* (cipher office) knew that too much information carried on one key was an advantage to the would-be code-breaker, so keys were changed more often – 1936 saw a move from quarterly wheel changes to monthly, and later in that year, daily. Likewise, the number of plugboard connections was increased.

On 15 September 1938, the day Chamberlain flew to Munich for a meeting with Hitler, the Enigma procedures were changed again. This time the ground setting was no longer printed in the instructions but a setting was chosen by the cipher clerk. This ended those so-convenient correspondences between first and fourth, second and fifth, etc., indicator letters. Amazingly, however, the Poles, resilient as ever, came back with the discovery that repetitions of indicator letters, with pairs of the *same* letter were occasionally to be found. (If JCBJCB were enciphered as BQROMR, the repeated 'R' would make the pair.) These were known as 'females'.[2]

All these changes made life much more difficult for the little Polish Cipher Bureau with its three mathematicians and small team of cipher clerks. To help exploit these elusive new pairings Zygalski developed the use of perforated sheets as an aid to tracking down the settings they wanted; and to eliminate the very large numbers of unwanted! When the sheets were passed over each other and corresponding holes were revealed by shining a light through them, a matching pair might be obtained. But these were very slow to make and tedious to use. Hard-pressed for staff, time and money, they then developed a machine that would do the job.

It consisted of six Enigma machines wired up in such a way that an electrical circuit would close if three matching pairs had been found. Perhaps due to its ticking noise it was called a 'Bombe'.[3] Although a fairly straightforward machine, designed for a limited purpose, the Bombe pointed the way forward, a first step along the road that would lead, within two years, to a sophisticated machine that would greatly assist deciphering at Bletchley Park: the Turing-Welchman Bombe, the machine that would play an important part in helping to shorten the War.

# Impasse

Although French Intelligence continued to supply the Poles with copies of stolen documents obtained by their agent, the Poles, according to Bertrand, gave absolutely nothing but gratitude in return. No deciphered documents, no information gleaned from German wireless transmissions, were ever handed over. The French must have concluded that the Poles were as much in the dark as they were, or they were keeping very quiet for fear of annoying the Germans, with whom they had a non-aggression treaty. The French authorities, nonetheless, thought it prudent to continue to supply material to the Poles right up to the middle of 1938, when, as a result of the vast German military expansion their spy, Hans-Thilo Schmidt, transferred to other duties at the end of September.

France in the 1920s had regarded Poland as a military counter-weight to any future threat from Germany, and the Polish Army, in those days, was considerably larger than the German. But Hitler's frantic rearmament in the mid-1930s changed the situation completely, although the French probably found it extremely hard to accept the big shift in the balance of power that this implied.

The Polish Cipher Bureau, which had its Bombe working by November 1938, found its usefulness dramatically cut short. Suddenly, in the middle of December, they could no longer read German wireless Enigma traffic, not even partially or occasionally. They soon realized what had happened. The Germans had increased the number of wheels for each machine from three to a choice of three out of five. The wheels were removable as before, and still had to be placed in a different order each day, but now the total possible number of wheel orders was sixty instead of six. They would have needed sixty Bombes and more manpower. Their limited resources were outstripped. At that point the Poles were defeated after having had their best year for results.

At this moment of impasse, a conference was due to be called in Paris attended by cipher experts from Britain, France and Poland. The Poles fervently hoped that one of the others would have something to offer but were instructed to give nothing away unless progress with Enigma had been made by the British or French and they were prepared to say so. Alas, neither had anything to offer; the British because they had not yet employed a mathematician – the pre-war British Secret Service was believed to have an innate dislike of university men – the French failure being just as shameful, as the stolen documents had been passing through their hands for six years!

## A wonderful gift – just in the nick of time!

The Munich Agreement (which Churchill described as a 'defeat without a war') had ceded to Germany the Sudetenland part of Czechoslovakia, thus allowing German troops to march unopposed through the very strong, deep defences the Czechs had built along the German border. The leading German generals, knowing the defences, and the well-organized and well-armed Czech army, were prepared to remove Hitler at that point, it is now revealed, rather than fight a protracted war exposing a German Army not yet fully-trained and equipped. However, it was obvious to everyone except the Chamberlain and Daladier governments, that Hitler would soon occupy the rest of Czechoslovakia despite his solemn assurances to the contrary. This he did in March 1939, and finally convinced the wavering British and French that he was bent on conquest and on changing the whole balance of power. Czechoslovakia and its system of alliances with France and Russia had been the only real military obstacle; now the whole of Europe lay at Hitler's feet. The British and French responded to the invasion of Czechoslovakia by giving Poland guarantees in the event of an un-provoked attack by Germany. Hitler immediately renounced the 1934 Non-Aggression Treaty with Poland, and this was followed by a deaf-ening propaganda campaign which soon escalated into violence with bombs exploding in Polish homes, and numerous incidents instigated or manufactured to inflame the situation. The local Nazis in Danzig behaved as though they were the occupying power. This extremely tense and deteriorating situation finally removed any lingering doubts the Poles may have had about informing Britain and France, now their allies, about their deciphering achievements. The British and French were invited to a meeting in Warsaw on 24 July 1939. The British party comprised Denniston, Knox and Commander Humphrey Sandwith (head of naval interception and direction-finding), transformed in some books into Colonel Menzies, deputy head of SIS, posing as 'Professor Sandwich', an Oxford mathematician! There they were shown, to their utter amazement, the Polish-built Enigma machines, the perforated sheets and the Bombe. Then in an act of enormous generosity, the Poles

21

offered an Enigma machine to each of their allies, together with drawings of the Zygalski sheets and the Bombe, all of which reached London on 16 August, two weeks before Hitler's sudden invasion of Poland.

## Postscript – red faces!

Warsaw proved a big eye-opener for the British party. What had particularly exasperated Dillwyn Knox, the veteran GC&CS code-breaker, who had applied himself, without success, to the solution of the German military Enigma, was how, 'the letters of the keyboard were connected to the twenty-six input discs (contacts) of the entry plate[4] . . . it was obvious to us [recounts Peter Twinn, who helped Knox during the last few months before the War] that the Germans would take advantage of the immense number of possible random orders from which they could choose.'[5] They could have done, they certainly should have done – but they didn't! As Peter Twinn says, 'the number of ways of ordering twenty-six letters is an unimaginable number, more than twenty digits long.'[6] The German designers, however, had simply connected keyboard to entry plate in a perfectly straightforward order, so that Q W E R T Z U etc.,[7] the order of the keyboard, became just A B C D E F G etc., a quite amazing oversight, not to say downright blunder, on the part of the German designers back in the late 1920s. Of course, boffins like Twinn would never have ignored such an opportunity. The trouble was, they couldn't imagine anyone else doing so! As Twinn remarks, it 'provided a distinguished Polish cryptanalyst [code-breaker] with a glorious bull's eye, and gave us the opportunity of recording our feeblest performance'.[8]

Twinn much regrets not seeing what 'in retrospect seems such a reasonable possibility' and – as he had been given a long enciphered message complete with its (supposed) plaintext original (probably obtained by a spy) – he might have been reading messages within a fortnight of his arrival, and thus 'made a debut of unparalleled brilliance'.[9] In his own defence he points out that not only he, but Knox, Kendrick and Turing also missed what was under their very noses. Finally, the long message turned out to be genuine.

Hans-Thilo Schmidt was finally betrayed, then arrested and shot by the Germans in July 1943. He was not a man opposed to the Nazi regime; indeed he had joined the Nazi Party before 1933 (Membership No. 738736). He simply spied for monetary reward and the restored status money would bring. For all that, he is a man to whom the wartime Allies, and the many millions who were hoping for an Allied victory, have to be eternally grateful.

The Polish contribution to the Enigma story, regrettably, has been the subject of controversy. Some Polish writers have claimed too much, and some British, including official historians, have sought to belittle their achievement. Essentially, the Poles, just in the nick of time, showed that the impossible was possible, that the 'unbreakable' Enigma system could, after all, be broken. If the Polish equipment had not arrived at Bletchley Park when it did, they would not have obtained their initial successes early in 1940, and would have been unable to demonstrate to sceptical and even hostile admirals, generals and Whitehall mandarins, that deciphering his signals was a wonderfully accurate way of gaining information about the enemy when all other sources had closed. Had they not been in a position to do this, it is extremely doubtful whether a single central intelligence organization would ever have emerged. Indeed, in all likelihood, code-breaking would have reverted to the three separate armed services, traditionally jealous of the code-breakers now at Bletchley Park and of each other. Just to underline the sheer awfulness of the situation one has to recall that at this time British knowledge of the enemy – his armament, military and industrial strength and potential – was, in a word, abysmal!

Before leaving the subject of the remarkable Polish gift, it should be noted that simply possessing an Enigma machine together with its wheel wirings, does not, in itself, enable one to break ciphers. There remains the problem of breaking the daily keys – ways of setting it up – of which the design of the machine provided a quite astronomical number. These instruction keys were changed daily (later in the War twice daily), and yet somehow this mind-boggling number of possibilities had to be reduced to manageable proportions, and on a daily basis. This is why the gift of the Zygalski sheets – enabling Bletchley to make a complete set – was just as important as that of the machine itself. With these perforated sheets it might have been said, 'The impossible we do immediately!'

## Notes

1. The day's batch of messages would often yield enough repeats of indicator letters already used to enable them to find a pattern and then build up a complete table.

23

2. Without a common ground setting and with the new three-letter wheel setting chosen by the clerk openly announced in the preamble to the message, security of the system depended upon the common ring setting which was changed daily. If the Poles could find enough clues ('female' pairs) in the messages the ring setting could be deduced.
3. French for 'bomb' – might have originated in a popular Polish ice-cream, the 'Bomba'.
4. The entry plate was one of two fixed wheels or plates and three revolving wheels (US 'rotors'), which comprised the 'scrambler unit' (Welchman's term) of the Enigma machine.
5. *Codebreakers, the Inside Story of Bletchley Park*, edited by F.H. Hinsley and Alan Stripp (Oxford, OUP, 1993), p. 126.
6. Ibid.
7. As on the standard German typewriter keyboard.
8. Hinsley and Stripp, *Codebreakers*, p. 125.
9. Ibid., p. 127.

# Chapter 3

# THE IMPOSSIBLE WE DO
# IMMEDIATELY . . .

## Success and Expansion at Bletchley Park

Regardless of the generally chaotic condition of British Intelligence at
the outbreak of war in 1939, advantage was not taken of the respite
afforded by the 'Phoney War' period which lasted from September 1939
to April 1940. Except that in a quiet corner of England, at Bletchley
Park in Buckinghamshire, the new wartime home of GC&CS, things
were beginning to move. New recruits (those in the know) felt an air of
excitement following the gift of equipment and documents from Poland
which had reached Bletchley just a few weeks earlier. Denniston had
recruited from his emergency list an initial intake of up to twenty 'men
of the Professor type', of whom, however, only three were mathematicians. As it transpired, these three, Alan Turing, Gordon Welchman and
John Jeffreys, among the cream of Cambridge mathematicians at that
time, could be said to have 'fathered' the new organization, Station X,
as it became known to the intelligence community – Bletchley Park, or
BP, or 'the Park', to the thousands who worked there during the War.
Although it became a veritable aristocracy of the talents, with the pick
of British brains being recruited in goodly numbers, and the whole place
exerting a huge collective effort, these three filled their individual bills
to perfection.

The war-scare at the time of the Munich 'Agreement' in September
1938 having begun to concentrate a few minds, GC&CS, at long, long

last, recognized that tackling machine ciphers like those of the German Enigma was a job for mathematicians, and short courses were held at Broadway Buildings. All three men had attended these; Turing, who had a special interest in 'machine computation', later 'helped out' occasionally at weekends during 1938/39.

Bletchley Park was a medium-sized manor house of unappealing aspect standing in modest grounds near the railway town of Bletchley, fifty miles north-west of London and very convenient for both Oxford and Cambridge. It turns out to have been purchased, not by the British Government, but by Hugh Sinclair, head of the Secret Intelligence Service, an act of far-sighted wisdom for which the hard-pressed war-time Allies should be very grateful.

What Bletchley Park did in the autumn of 1939 was to start where the Poles had been compelled to stop. As mentioned previously, the German changes at the end of 1938 left them defeated only by lack of resources and manpower. The number of wheels of the Enigma machine had been increased from three – giving six possible positions in which they could be arranged – to a choice of three out of five, giving sixty! The little Polish Cipher Bureau had even been clever enough to work out the wiring of the new wheels because the SD (*Sicherheitsdienst*), the Nazi Party intelligence agency and part of the SS, were slow to implement the new system and the Poles were able to intercept messages in both new and old systems at the same time (probably receiving the same message in both systems). But it availed them nothing for they would have needed sixty Bombes and a great many more perforated sheets which would have vastly exceeded their small budget. Even if they had been in a position to cope with this greatly increased requirement, the further German changes, in January 1939, increasing the number of plugboard connections from seven pairs to ten, would have much reduced the capacity of the Polish Bombe.

The new BP recruits therefore (not yet having a 'Bombe' of their own), set about the daunting task of making sixty sets of twenty-six perforated sheets, which involved checking over one million combinations of wheel and ring settings! Large numbers of very precisely placed holes had to be punched in the sheets, although once made they could be used as an essential deciphering tool on a daily basis. A detailed description of Gordon Welchman's own design for perforated sheets is to be found in his book, *The Hut Six Story*,[1] and this is probably similar to the one actually used. In any case, it is all we have. Welchman describes how, in October 1939, while ostensibly working on traffic analysis at BP, some of which he had been able to delegate to young assistants, he worked out his perforated, or punched-hole, sheet system, and proudly offered it to Dillwyn Knox. A former classicist, plagued with serious illness, brusque and secretive, Knox was still in charge of the 'attack' on the Enigma against which after years of work he had made no progress whatsoever. A little while earlier he had removed Welchman from the Enigma team after only a week or two, and was less than over-joyed to find his traffic analysis man offering solutions to fundamental problems. 'Dilly was furious. What I was suggesting was precisely what he was already doing, and the necessary sheets were already being punched under the direction of my Cambridge friend and colleague, John Jeffreys.'[2]

Although it might be justified by Bletchley's 'need to know' rule (roughly, if you don't have a compelling reason for wanting to know, based on your own work, don't ask!) possibly being applied in those very early days, it is astonishing that a brilliant mathematician like Welchman should not know of developments taking place within a stone's throw of where he was working. In this case it is evident that Knox simply disliked Welchman. To add to the distaste of many classi-cists towards mathematicians, there was likely to have been a clash of personalities. Knox, who liked to make mysteries, speak in riddles and then exhibit impatience with those who failed to understand him, would not have taken to this newcomer who would have ideas of his own, organizational as well as technical, and would not be slow in advancing them.

## Academic with 'fire in his belly'

Welchman was in fact somewhat unusual for an academic at the time, in that he foresaw, even at that very early stage, how a major code-breaking organization could be set up, and was also a man of courage, with sufficient 'fire in his belly' to persuade the authorities first to listen, and then not only be convinced that his ideas were essential, but really to act along the lines he had suggested.

Gordon Welchman, then aged thirty-four, had won a mathematics scholarship to Trinity College, Cambridge in 1925, and was made a Research Fellow at Sidney Sussex College in 1929. He continued to teach mathematics at Cambridge until the War in 1939, his special field being algebraic geometry. Described as having 'dashing good looks with dark wavy hair', he was considered a 'solemn old stick' by some of his colleagues. Welchman is a pivotal figure in the establishing of Bletchley Park as we know it, and any discussion of the basic organization and initial success of Bletchley must emphasize his role. His book, already referred to, first published in 1982, was a landmark in the history of British code-breaking; his clear, detailed descriptions of how it was actually done blowing away many of the cobwebs of half-truth, distortion and exaggeration that had begun to obscure these developments, the long official secrecy having prevented an agreed account of the subject. In charge of Hut Six, the great power house of Bletchley in the early years, Welchman was promoted in 1943 to be Assistant Director for Mechanisation.

Astonishingly, Welchman, who worked for many years in the United States after the War, and who had become an American citizen, was censured, and even threatened with legal action by the security authorities for revealing too much detail in his book about how the Enigma system was actually broken, notwithstanding that this was forty years after the event, at a time when modern computers had long consigned wartime ciphering machines to the museum.

## Breaking the unbreakable

As soon as the perforated sheets had been completed, copies were sent to the Château de Vignolles, a country house some thirty miles northeast of Paris where members of the Polish Cipher Bureau had joined the French under Bertrand after managing to escape the Nazi invasion of Poland. The British 'emissary' who took the sheets was almost certainly Alan Turing, although his biographer did not think this was a job for a 'man of the professor type'. In fact, Turing would have been the very person to deal with any problems that may have arisen. In the event the 'emissary' returned in January 1940 with the very exciting news that an enemy key for 28 October 1939 had been broken using Bletchley's sheets. This turned out to be traffic from within the twenty German home military districts, which Welchman had labelled 'Green', and was the first wartime breaking of an enemy key. It was a tremendous achievement and caused BP to bend every effort to equal and, if possible, better the Franco-Polish result. But things were not going so well in other parts of the intelligence community. During the first months of the War the Secret Service (SIS) was being roundly condemned by the three service intelligence divisions for its failure to provide them with good information about the German enemy. In fact, most of the SIS network of European agents had been broken up or had disintegrated at the outbreak of the war, and no secure 'stay-behind' organization had been created – all part of the general British unpreparedness. SIS was then dealt another blow by the unexpected death in November 1939 of its Chief, Admiral Sinclair, who in many ways 'was' the SIS. This news was compounded when, a few days later, two of their most senior agents, Best and Stevens, men with extensive knowledge of British networks and contacts abroad, were led into a trap at Venlo on the Dutch/German border and kidnapped by the Germans, having recently passed some of their latest wireless equipment to a German 'agent' who turned out to be a member of the SD (Nazi Party intelligence). SIS's stock in Whitehall was at a very low ebb.

The news from Paris thus came as a heaven-sent relief to the hard-pressed Stewart Menzies, Sinclair's deputy, the new head of SIS and of course, of GC&CS at Bletchley Park. Work at BP was now commenced on another German intercepted message, that for 25 October, also a 'Green', and this was broken at the beginning of January 1940, to be followed shortly afterwards by breaking the Luftwaffe general key, which Welchman had dubbed 'Red'.

## You can't keep a good man down!

Let us then return to Gordon Welchman and his traffic analysis. He had been asked, specifically, to study 'call-signs and discriminants'. Being the sort of man he was he couldn't easily be fobbed off with routine work, and Knox's spleen, or whatever, in ejecting him from the Enigma team, was to have several important consequences. After being shown some of the very few deciphered messages in Bletchley's possession, Welchman began to see, as he says, at first, 'somewhat dimly'[3] that he was involved not so much in trying to disentangle single messages, of 'solving intricate puzzles',[4] but with an entire 'communications system that would serve the needs of the German ground and air forces.'[5] Welchman began to realize that the German fighting formations would each be served by a signals detachment which would operate a wireless network on an allocated frequency. The wireless stations which made up the network could be some distance apart, and in theory they should be able to hear each other. Stations would act in turn as the 'control' whose job was to ensure that no two stations were transmitting at the same time and to ensure that the stations in the network were 'alive and well'. This the controller did by calling them up and engaging in a certain amount of 'chit-chat' at intervals of about twelve hours. It was only in extreme circumstances that the Germans could maintain complete wireless silence. In practice, enemy short-wave communication was constantly bedevilled by problems of fading and frequency drifting, and this generated 'chit-chat' as the controllers struggled to keep their networks open.

Welchman points out in his book that there were many of these wireless networks, serving different parts of the German fighting machine, and that an individual wireless station could 'operate in two or more (networks) so that messages originating at any one point could be relayed to any other point.' When messages were sent between two stations in the same network the plain language preamble to the message would carry the call signs of the sender and the intended receiver. If a message had to be relayed to other stations the preamble would include the call signs of both the originator and the two (or more) recipients of the message (e.g. G5Z to KGG and 4QK). Studying call signs was one way of finding out something of the structure of the German forces. The problem, however, was that call signs were changed daily, so daily analysis was a continuing task.

Welchman realized that the form filled in by the British operators at the listening stations must have been very similar to those used by the German Enigma clerks. The preamble, transmitted in plain language, would have been taken down by the British operator, except that he or she would have preceded it with the frequency to which they were listening and the time of interception. The preamble (see Appendix 2 for details) would have been followed by the enciphered six-letter indicator and then the rest of the message. At that point, of course, the enciphered messages were of no particular interest to Welchman (the Enigma ciphers had not yet been broken) so he began to log the details of each day's traffic (from the interception station at Chatham) by frequency and time of interception. He also took other details from the preamble including the call sign, time of origin and the *Kenngruppen* to which Bletchley gave the truly awful name of 'discriminants'. This was a set of four three-letter groups which was printed under the last column in the daily set of instructions for setting up the

Enigma machine. It was essential information, as we shall see, but did not form part of the operating instructions. The set of letters designated a particular group of users, e.g. those entitled to use the SS key, or the air force general key – each group would be issued with the same printed sheets of operating instructions every month. Thus 'key' had two meanings: general, for a group of users, and particular, for today's operating instructions.

## Welchman uncovers an enemy weakness

Hitler was always suspicious that other centres of power might emerge within the Reich and one way to prevent this was to limit access to information by any one body, and the influence or power that knowledge might bring. Accordingly, the army, for example, would not have access to SS messages, and therefore, had their own key. But messages of different types were often sent on the same wireless network. The problem was overcome by the clerk sending the message using a three-letter 'discriminant' which selected or 'discriminated' between the various keys in use. This three-letter 'code' was openly announced in the plain-language preamble to the message, and told the receiving clerk at the outset which key was being used on this occasion. If he had been issued with the key denoted he could go ahead and set up his machine in the same way as that of the sending clerk, and so be able to decipher the message. Without that key he could not proceed.

In searching the preambles of the daily batch of intercepts for their discriminants, Welchman realized that if a long message, say a four-part message, were being sent, all four of the three-letter groups were being used. Welchman knew that a four-part message going to the same addressee must be enciphered in the same key, so all the discriminants must belong to the same set of four. This was an enemy blunder, because only one of the three-letter groups should have been used for all four parts of the message. What Welchman had to do was to examine the day's traffic for a four-part message to know that he had identified the key in use. Once deciphering started this would prove a great asset, provided no mistake was made. At first he was able to pick out three keys, which he marked with red, green and blue pencils. Thus began Bletchley's naming system for enemy keys, and one, the Red, became the most famous of all. He also analysed the 'back-traffic', old intercepts still on file, for call-sign repeats and was able to

31

give the listening station at Chatham a useful forecast of those to be expected. Although call signs and discriminants seemed innocuous at the time, Welchman brought them to life, and they were the means of making contact with Chatham, and getting on good terms with Commander Ellingworth, who was in charge, and, 'who taught me a great many things I badly needed to know'.[6] From him Welchman learned how German wireless networks operated and about the problems of interception. For example, the phenomenon of 'fading', although a great nuisance to those attempting to listen to and log Morse code signals, was actually a wonderful boon. Because short-wave transmissions are reflected from the upper atmosphere, signals can cover considerable distances. It is because of this that fairly low-powered short-wave transmitters, as used in field conditions to send Enigma messages, could be received, although not without difficulty, in the British Isles. Again, short-wave frequencies tended to 'drift', and interception operators – a race of unsung war heroes who did long stints, commonly six hours – buried in headphones, tried desperately to disentangle often weak signals from the 'snap, crackle and pop' which accompanied them. Their keenness and dedication was in marked contrast to the indifference and sloppiness exhibited by some operators on the enemy side, especially in the Luftwaffe, where General Martini complained of the quality of the signals staff. Drifting would cause problems when the frequency to which an operator was listening actually disappeared and he or she would have to retune with the greatest care. Similarly, if they were asked to log a network using a specific frequency, they might all too easily find themselves listening to another network on a very closely neighbouring frequency. Many operators developed their listening skills to an astonishingly high level, able to detect weak signals, recognize the characteristics of particular enemy networks and even the style or 'fist' of a particular operator. Naturally, all the operators were convinced that all the messages were being decoded. In order to try and offset the effects of fading and drifting, interception stations controlled by BP were often double banked, so that what was blank or corrupt in one station's report might be clear in another's.

The attempts, sometimes desperate, of the German controllers to keep their wireless networks working – making contact, following traffic procedures with queries, permission, requests, etc. – resulted in much 'chit-chat' involving repeated call signs and much use of a version of the international 'Q-Code' (three-letter groups beginning with 'Q') all of which helped British listeners to keep track of particular stations and networks.

## Notes

1. Welchman, G., *The Hut Six Story* (Cleobury Mortimer, Baldwin, 1997).
2. Ibid. p. 71.
3. Ibid. p. 38.
4. Ibid.
5. Ibid.
6. Ibid. p. 55.

# Chapter 4

# HUT SIX –
# WHERE IT ALL BEGAN

Later on, from Hut Six's Interception Control Room BP would direct the attention of interception stations to those networks which were likely to carry the most important intelligence. The upshot of Welchman's liaison with Chatham was that information about all intercepted Enigma traffic was sent to BP where a traffic register was established.[1] This was sent by teleprinter as groups of messages were intercepted. In return, Welchman agreed to telephone Chatham each day as soon as he had identified a set of discriminants, e.g. Red or Blue, together with a prediction of call signs to be used which would be of help to the hard-pressed operators. With these rudimentary notions of a Registration Room and an Interception Control Room, Hut Six organization begins to take shape.

The late autumn of 1939 was in the 'Phoney War' period which lasted until the invasion of Denmark and Norway in April 1940. Welchman was well aware that the perforated sheets being produced by Jeffreys and his team would probably soon result in a break into the German Enigma traffic, but that the people around him were thinking in terms of deciphering success and nothing more. He also knew that the Phoney War was but a breathing space before the 'hot war' began, and he foresaw that in order to exploit the very extensive use which he expected the enemy to make of the Enigma system, code-breaking success would mean organization on a scale hitherto undreamt of. More interception stations needed to be established and at widely dispersed locations, so that stations might be twinned or double banked as mentioned

34

previously. Particularly would it be valuable if the nine 'indicator' letters (the last three of the preamble and the first six of the enciphered message) could be received by two operators, preferably some distance apart, to help ensure they were accurately received. This called, not only for rapid expansion, but for close co-ordination by BP. 'At that time I myself was the only co-ordinator, and self-appointed at that, and I was dealing with only one interception station.'[2] He also envisaged rapid expansion of the small traffic analysis effort he had started if the interception facilities were to be enlarged as he hoped.

In addition to Registration and Control (of interception) Welchman planned a Machine Room occupied by the code-breakers themselves centred around a Watch, and they would work closely with the other two rooms. Then there would be a Sheet-stacking Room where the punched-hole sheets could be manipulated, and whose assistance the Machine Room would request when the possibility of breaking a key appeared, and a Decoding Room equipped with British Type-X cipher machines adapted for use as Enigma machines so that possible breaks could be tested and broken keys deciphered.[3] The broken key would yield the instructions for setting up the Enigma machine that the original sender of the message had used; now the Hut Six machines would be set up in exactly the same way. Finally, Welchman thought all five sections should go on to three-shift, 24-hour working, as soon as possible, and two of them even before the perforated sheets were finished.

This was the scheme presented by Welchman to Commander Edward Travis, the deputy head of BP, whose response was very positive. In retrospect it seems quite incredible that a newcomer, an academic and a civilian, with hardly any experience of what was in any case a minor branch of the school's work (traffic analysis), should offer this overweeningly ambitious, seemingly madcap, scheme to a hardened administrator used to working within narrowly-prescribed limits and on a very tight budget, and perhaps even more incredible, that he should accept. But this is to underrate the two men. Travis could see that here was no ordinary academic, but a very down-to-earth organizer, a practical visionary, and undoubtedly Welchman's arguments would have been very convincing. Travis was probably anxious that the new venture at Bletchley Park should succeed; there was certainly no shortage of ambitious service organizations willing or wishing to take it over or absorb it. Denniston, the head of BP, was known to be ineffectual, and if changes had to be made, now was the time, with all British institutions reeling from the sudden imposition of wartime conditions and requirements, a chaotic period in which there were few new rules and no one quite knew who was who or what was what. For all that, it was a great act of faith, the punched-hole or perforated sheets still unfinished and no wartime Enigma message yet broken.

## Laying the groundwork

The project went ahead rapidly; approval was quickly obtained from those at Bletchley with Denniston, Colonel Tiltman, head of the Army section and Josh Cooper, of the Air Force section, accepting that the new arrangements would be on an inter-service basis. Recruiting of personnel went forward with many personal contacts of former college students, colleagues and so on, the unreliability of such methods offset by the impossibility of explaining the nature of the work so that the recruit put his or her trust in a person they knew, while those recruiting had a fair idea of the abilities and qualities needed for this very unusual type of work.

'In winning approval of this plan at so early a date,' Welchman claims, 'I probably made my biggest single contribution to the war effort.'[4]

From January 1940, breaking the German Air Force key, the 'Red', was accomplished fairly frequently, often in the early hours, not long after the keys were changed at midnight. Responsibility for the five sections of Hut Six was divided between Welchman, who was in charge of interception control, registration and decoding, with John Jeffreys in charge of sheet stacking and the Machine Room. In the four months that followed a great deal was learned about enemy Enigma procedure and the habits of the operators, especially the Luftwaffe, whose Blue key often produced nothing more than whimsical material such as nursery rhymes for the signals units in training. Although there was little hard intelligence, the period was of the utmost value in discovering how the Enigma system operated, its strengths and its weaknesses. Eventually, more traffic began to emerge from north Germany, probably training signallers for the coming invasion of Denmark and Norway in April. For this campaign, referred to previously, the Germans used a new combined operations key, labelled 'Yellow' at BP, which was broken some five days after the invasion of Norway on

10 April. It yielded a great wealth of intelligence material which, tragically, the British were in no position to use.

Then, in May 1940, disaster struck. What happened was that a huge German procedural blunder, which had enabled first the Poles, and then the British, to break into the 'impregnable' German Enigma traffic, was at last rectified, to coincide with the 'blitzkrieg' invasion of western Europe. As already mentioned, the three Enigma indicator letters were enciphered twice, and these six letters formed the first part of the enciphered message. This double encipherment – intended to make certain that the receiving clerk had received the indicator letters absolutely correctly – had provided a way into the system that the Poles were quick to exploit. The code-breakers knew that in a six-letter group, the first and fourth letters were enciphered versions of the same original letter. (If JCBJCB had been enciphered by the machine as BQROMP, both B and O would be versions of J.) The same applies to the second and fifth, and to the third and sixth letters. Even after September 1938, when German procedural changes did away with these very convenient pairings of first and fourth etc. indicator letters, the Poles found new pairings, this time of indicator letters which *were* actually the *same*, although much harder to exploit, and developed aids, such as perforated sheets, and even a machine – the 'Bombe' – to help reduce the workload. The British perforated sheets performed the same function and worked well,[5] but still based, of course, on that double encipherment of the indicator letters; and the Hut Six boffins knew that if the enemy discontinued that arrangement they would be in trouble. They were! Certainly, the Turing-Welchman Bombe, unlike the Polish original, did not depend on double encipherment, and was altogether more advanced, but it was still in the prototype stage and would not be ready for months. Thus the perforated sheets, so recently made after months of very painstaking work, were suddenly useless, and Welchman's slick new organization faced a crisis with the German attack just about to begin.

With the double encipherment of the indicator letters gone, the perforated sheets rendered obsolete, and the Bombe still in the experimental stage, Welchman and his team gazed into the abyss. How would they, how could they, hang on? Was it Churchill who once mentioned 'a mystery inside an enigma'? A gap of even a few months with loss of continuity and unable to keep up with enemy changes may have prevented them from ever catching up. And their erstwhile efforts

37

notwithstanding, they badly needed to build up a substantial bank of cribs against the day when the first Bombe came on stream. No cribs, no Bombe; it was that simple.

But they had made the best possible use of their deciphering Luftwaffe Red and Blue keys in the period January to May. They had studied German procedures very closely, as well as the habits of cipher clerks, looking constantly for weaknesses – and finding them! Hut Six labelled two of these weaknesses the 'Herivel tip' and 'Sillies'; the first enabled them to guess the Enigma wheel ring settings to within two or three letters, the second to guess text settings.[6] Both became sufficiently common to be usable in code-breaking when the enemy cipher clerks had to work under pressure after the invasion of 10 May.

John Herivel, one of Welchman's former bright maths students, now in Hut Six, imagined how a lazy cipher clerk might save himself trouble when setting up the machine for the new key each day. The clerk would first choose the correct three wheels, then set the alphabet ring on each wheel, place the wheels in the correct order in the machine and shut the lid.

> To set an alphabet ring on a wheel, he would probably hold the wheel in one hand so that the clip position was facing him, and then rotate the ring until the correct letter was opposite the clip position. Then the clip would engage. Herivel's contribution was to realise that, when the operator inserted the wheel into the machine, the letter determining the ring setting would probably still be facing him, and when he closed the cover it was quite likely that the three letters appearing in the [little windows] would be pretty close to the ring settings of the new key. Indeed, if the operator was lazy he might leave the wheels in their initial positions when he encoded his text setting for his first message of the day. If so, the letters of the indicator setting in the preamble of this message would be pretty close to the ring settings in the new key.[7]

Promptly, the Hut Six Machine Room Watch, searching their traffic registers soon after midnight for the newly intercepted messages, would look for indicator settings in the preambles to Red key messages. They would be entered in a specially designed 'Herivel square', and if a cluster of three-letter indicators began to appear in a portion of the square, the boffins would be able to hazard a shrewd guess as to what the day's ring settings might be.[8] As Welchman says, 'the 17,576 possible ring settings had been reduced to six probables.' A master stroke of applied psychology! (In order to break a key – one day's setting-up instructions – the code-breakers needed to discover: the wheel-order; ring settings; cross-pluggings; and text setting.)

It might be helpful to summarize the Enigma procedure. The cipher clerk sending the message, after setting up his machine according to printed instructions (wheel order, ring settings, cross-pluggings)[9] chose three letters at random – plucked out of the air – say, JEF, and turned his wheels until those letters appeared in the little windows – this was the indicator setting (given in the preamble to tell the receiving clerk to do the same). He then chose a further three random letters (say, JCB, which was the text setting) and these three were tapped out on the keyboard twice (JCBJCB) which would be enciphered by the machine as six other letters (e.g. BQROMP) and these, known as the indicator, became the first six letters of the actual enciphered message.

The procedural changes already referred to were made just before the Germans invaded Western Europe in May 1940, when they either realized the enormity of their own blunder in the double encipherment of the text setting (JCBJCB), or simply tightened up the procedure on the eve of major military operations. We may never know, but in May, when the double encipherment was dropped, the indicator setting (e.g. JEF) and now the indicator (reduced from BQROMP to BQR, the result of tapping JCB once only) were both openly proclaimed in the plain-language (i.e. unenciphered) preamble. These preambles with their messages were, as usual, intercepted and teleprinted to BP, where the absence of the second set of three letters (OMP above) struck cold fear into the hearts of the Hut Six boffins.

Then came the very appropriate use of the 'Herivel tip', and hopes began to rise. The detailed knowledge of the practice and habits of Luftwaffe cipher clerks acquired over the previous months now bore even more fruit. A new discovery was made of such a bad habit that it was dubbed 'Sillies' or 'Cillis', but which, whatever its origin, speaks for itself. It might equally have been labelled 'idles'. Briefly, what happened was this. Enigma messages were limited, for security reasons, to 250 letters; a longer message would have to be sent in parts, each with its own preamble. As already mentioned, after the changes made in May 1940,[10] the preambles contained both indicator settings and indicators. For example, for a two-part message, the BP traffic register might show the letters WSX KMG as indicator setting and indicator for the first part of the message, and RFV LMS as setting and indicator for the second part. A quick glance at the Enigma keyboard (below) will show that the clerk, too idle even to pluck letters from the air, had simply selected the downward diagonal WSX, and the alternate one, RFV. The wizards of Hut Six would then surmise that he had chosen as his text settings the alternate downward diagonals EDC and TGB.

| Q | W | E | R | T | Z | U | I | O |
|---|---|---|---|---|---|---|---|---|
| A | S | D | F | G | H | J | K |   |
| P | Y | X | C | V | B | N | M | L |

But the supposition would have to be proved. The indicator letters are really the text setting, but disguised (enciphered) by the machine when the sending clerk tapped them out on the keyboard.

Detective work based on these 'Sillies' would now go ahead, using their knowledge of the workings of the machine, their mathematical and language skills and even their knowledge of the habits of individual cipher clerks! 'Sillies' together with the 'Herivel tip' usually enabled Hut Six to break the daily Luftwaffe Red key until the Bombe arrived in September.

Welchman said it might be hard to believe but it did actually happen, and indeed, went on happening.

'Unbelievable' it certainly must have seemed at the time, and even now it must be rated as a very considerable achievement. 'Breaking the Red key for the day', however, involved a great deal of very demanding, painstaking and usually nail-biting work. The 'Herivel tip' combined with the 'Sillies' were starting points, footholds: the mountain still had to be climbed, and again, and again, every single day, as the enemy changed his keys daily, at midnight.

In broad terms the task was to study the traffic registers looking for clues to ring settings (Herivel tips) and text settings (Sillies). When the watch leader thought he had a plausible set of guesses, he would prepare a menu (set of instructions) for the Decoding Room operators, who would go through the series of routines he specified on their modified Type-X machines [i.e. modified to serve as Enigma machines]. The process would be repeated for all the sixty possible wheel orders. Each such routine would produce a jumble of letters related to a particular combination of wheel order and ring settings. A visual inspection would sometimes indicate whether the combination could be consistent with the set of guesses on which the menu had been based. If the combination could not be discarded . . . further tests were carried out. If our guesses were correct, these tests would reveal the steckers [cross-pluggings], and we would have the complete key for the day. If all the menus . . . failed we simply had to try again.[11]

Sometimes all three watches failed to break the key – the Machine Room watches at that time, it should be noted, consisting of only two or three people.[12] If anyone reading the above summary feels that it doesn't sound too impossible, Welchman then invites his 'more technically minded' readers to consider some six pages where he gives a detailed explanation of the processes involved, and concludes,

Even when the German operators had given us a good Herivel tip and set of Sillies, the actual breaking of the key for the day involved a lot of work, in the course of which one could not afford to make any errors. Although the number of possibilities would have been reduced very considerably, one would still have to test for sixty possible wheel orders and quite a number of ring settings.[13]

## 'Sheer bloody guesswork'?

Even after finding the key for the day they were not necessarily 'home and dry'. The Decoding Room operator having set up her Type-X machine according to the newly-broken key did not always get German plain text. There could be a number of causes: faulty interception resulting in incorrect versions of the indicator setting or indicator (which might be rectified if there had been a second interception – if not she could check her list of common errors in Morse code interception, e.g. V confused with U, and try alternatives). Some messages would be flawed by fading signal strength or frequency drift in the wireless transmission leaving nasty gaps in the message. Again the Type-X operator would try and fill the gap – especially if the interception wireless operator had given an estimate of the number of five-letter groups thought to be missing. But time was always pressing and a partial decode would be sent to Hut Three who, if they thought it sufficiently important, would ask for the remainder to be decoded if possible.

It is said that there were only two ways of breaking into the Enigma:

faulty operating procedures; and failures to observe the rules. We saw a flagrant example of the first – the double encipherment – now closed; to be followed immediately by the second – cipher clerks flouting the rules and providing an opportunity for a break-in. May 1940 must have been an extremely anxious time, although very exciting too as enemy ciphers were broken with daring and ingenuity. 'Those first few days after the change on May 10 were quite fantastic,' Welchman recalls. 'Many people contributed bright ideas ... we were like a pack of hounds trying to pick up the scent.' Any gap in the code-breaking, 'lasted merely a few days' (from 14-20 May according to Welchman) and 'We were – though by a bare margin – still in the game.'[14]

One author, rather churlishly, has described all this as, 'sheer bloody guesswork'. Of course, 'ingenuity' and 'intuition' played their part, as in all code-breaking, and indeed, in a great deal of science – which often proceeds by 'hunches' and hypotheses which are then tested and modified in the light of experience. In May 1940 Hut Six's guesses were founded on previous experience, mathematics, language and psychology, as well as some bright ideas, and were nothing if not shrewd, well-informed and intelligent. 'Sheer guesswork', in the derogatory sense, might have served for a day or two, but from 22 May, the Red was broken every day, with very few exceptions, until the end of the War.

## Notes

1. At that stage Welchman did not require the intercepted message in full; all he needed was frequency and time of interception, followed by the plain language preamble (call signs, time of origin, indicator setting) and the first two enciphered groups which contained the six letters of the indicator. (See also Appendix 2.)
2. Welchman, *The Hut Six Story*, p. 74.
3. The 'Type-X' was originally a German commercial Enigma, modified by the British with certain attachments, and supplied to the Army and RAF from 1935.
4. Welchman, *The Hut Six Story*, p. 77.
5. If the volume of traffic using a particular key was able to produce enough indicator pairings – about one hundred messages might be enough to attack and probably break the key.
6. See Appendix 2.
7. Welchman, *The Hut Six Story*, pp. 98–9.
8. For further details see ibid. pp. 99–101.

9. See Appendix 2, also Hinsley and Stripp, *Codebreakers*, pp. 86–7.
10. The Official History, which was given exclusive access to certain records (which are otherwise to remain secret) of wartime intelligence activity, including Bletchley Park, gives 1 May as the date for 'new indicators for all Enigma keys, except the Yellow' in preparation for the invasion. Welchman, in *The Hut Six Story* gives 10 May – the invasion date – but later changes this to 15 May.
11. Welchman, *The Hut Six Story*, p. 104.
12. Watch leaders at this time included Stuart Milner-Barry (later Sir Stuart) who had played chess for England, and Dennis Babbage, a Cambridge mathematician.
13. Welchman, *The Hut Six Story*, p. 110.
14. Ibid. pp. 102–3.

# Chapter 5

# GUESSING WITH VIRTUAL CERTAINTY

## The Turing-Welchman Bombe

Despite the enhanced status, and indeed, survival, as an intelligence-gathering organization, that followed from the success of those early months of 1940, the real problem for GC&CS was not how to decipher messages sporadically, as was being done at that time, but somehow to get to grips with the entire enemy wireless communication system. At that point the enemy was still relying on his land-lines (Air Force Red and Blue traffic being an exception) but as Welchman had foreseen, when the hot war broke out, there would be a vast extension of wireless communication, and in the next twelve months, as the German war machine forced its way first into western and then southern Europe and the Soviet Union, there certainly was. This would mean dealing not with tens or even hundreds of signals a day, but with thousands. Only in that way, covering the whole wireless picture, reading a great deal of the enemy's secret military intelligence, would Bletchley Park make a major contribution to fighting and winning the War.

Small-scale deciphering, as the Poles had shown, and as Welchman and his team had demonstrated, could be done by 'hand methods', and after May 1940, as we have seen, even without perforated sheets.

Large-scale deciphering would require machinery, and so we come to the 'Bombe', designed by Turing and Welchman in 1939–40. As it happens, the considerable volume mentioned above as being necessary for BP's successful future, was in fact essential, both for the code-breakers, who would need a large amount of deciphered material 'under their belts' if they were to find enough 'cribs' to operate the Bombe, and also for the intelligence staff if they were to try and make sense of it all. The Bombe is useless without cribs and without a healthy body of previously deciphered material, cribs would not be found.

The idea behind the 'crib', as Bletchley called it, was the *mot probable*, the probable word, or phrase – i.e. anything which suggests that the message to be deciphered contains a certain phrase. This conjectured 'certain phrase' had to be matched against a portion of the enciphered message – the phrase slotted in to the exact position it would have occupied in the original plaintext message; something like a crazy crossword puzzle where you supply the clues, make up key words and imagine the rest. In other words the boffins were required to 'guess with virtual certainty' at least part of the content of the (still enciphered) original message. A tall order! The Bombe would then be used to test whether any Enigma wheel positions would allow for such a suggested encipherment. The Bombe was essentially a number of Enigma machines linked together which would run rapidly through a large number of possible wheel positions until an ingeniously designed test-register would signal a possible solution, and the machine would stop. The readings the machine produced would be settings – Enigma wheel positions – and these would be tested by setting up an Enigma machine at the positions indicated, tapping in the enciphered message, and seeing whether the result was in German, or gobbledygook, or a mixture of the two. If the result was complete nonsense the machine would have to be restarted with further adjustments until the correct wheel positions were found – or sometimes were not found. In fact failure, or long delay, was quite common with Turing's experimental Bombe (nicknamed 'Victory') which was in use from April or May 1940.

The big bugbear was how to cope with the Enigma plugboard. The number of ways of connecting ten pairs of letters – the number of plugboard connections the operators made (and changed every night) – is an awesome number some fifteen digits long. But mathematicians could reduce these to numbers manageable by the Bombe which was designed to work its way quickly through large numbers of possibilities. Results would partly depend on how it was set up – the instructions for the Bombe operators were in the form of a 'menu', which contained certain letters taken from the crib and chained together in the form of a 'loop'.

45

(Three loops were needed to avoid excessive delay and messages did not often yield cribs long enough to provide them.) A particular letter from the crib, designated the 'input letter', was fed in, and the Bombe and test register were then run through many wheel settings to see if one of the twenty-six plugboard partner letters of the input letter was consistent with the menu. If it were, the machine would automatically stop and readings would be taken. This would yield only a wheel setting and just one plugboard partner – hand-operated devices would then be used to see if from the one pair found by the Bombe the remaining pairs for the other menu letters could be elucidated. If not the machine would be restarted. In addition to these false stops the Bombe could also come to a stop by chance.

Joan Murray (then Joan Clarke), a young Cambridge mathematician[1] arrived in Hut Eight in June 1940, and recalls,

It was probably early in July 1940 . . . that Turing gave further consideration to 'simultaneous scanning' – that is, to finding a method of making the bombe test 26 hypotheses at each position of the wheels. Otherwise, the best one could do with the first British bombe . . . was to assume that the letter chosen for the input one was unplugged, with a possibility of 6 in 26 of this being correct. Turing soon jumped up, saying that Welchman's diagonal board would provide simultaneous scanning.[2]

It [the diagonal board] was a spectacular improvement; they no longer needed to look for 'loops' and so could make do with fewer and shorter cribs. With the addition of a diagonal board the Bombe would enjoy an almost uncanny elegance and power . . . With this fourfold proliferation of implications at every stage it became possible to use the Bombe on any 'crib' of three or four words. The analyst could select a 'menu' of some ten or so letters from the 'crib' sequence – not necessarily including a 'loop', but still as rich as possible in letters bound to lead to implications for other letters. And this would pose a very severe consistency condition, sweeping away billions of false hypotheses with the speed of light.[3]

Twenty-six times faster in operation, the Bombe could go through half a million wheel positions in hours rather than days. It had to be very well engineered, the wheels having to remain perfectly synchronized even after many hours of running at speed. The improved machine, incorporating three diagonal boards, comprised the equivalent of thirty-six Enigma machines (three banks of twelve on the face of the Bombe).

The first prototype of the Turing-Welchman Bombe, produced in months compared with years in peacetime, was delivered to Hut Eleven in August 1940 and went into service in September. It was nicknamed 'Agnus'.

How then did the 'wizards' of the Hut Six Watch, as Welchman called them, manage to fit conjectured plaintext to a portion of the enciphered message? Considering the fairly stereotyped nature of much military communication, finding cribs was not quite so difficult as it sounds. Among the many possible sources of cribs were: the results of previous solutions (including those of several enemy hand-ciphers broken at BP); fairly standard terminology used in plaintext preambles; radio-telephone 'chit-chat' (fighter planes, E-boats), all carefully logged; addresses; signatures; weather reports – often sent at regular intervals on known frequencies. Very useful indeed would be someone who reports every day that he has 'nichts zu melden', nothing to report.

```
KOMJS   LFOUR   HIEFA
NICHT   SZUME   LDEN
```

The above attempt at a crib would fail as the two 'E's in the third group clash; a weakness in the Enigma – and a boon to the code-breaker – being that no letter could ever go to itself.

Naturally, a very sharp lookout was kept for reciphered messages, i.e. the same message as sent previously but using a different key and which had already been deciphered. Being Bletchley, such gems were registered and carefully tracked as they went from one key to another or from one day to the next. An enormous amount of record-keeping was done – invaluable sources for the perplexed code-breaker. Needless to say good cribs were assiduously collected and indexed, any changes being noted.

The American code-breaker William F. Friedman, seeing several indexes of cribs during his visit to BP, wisecracked, 'Ah, not cryptography but cribography!'

## Enter the right firm at the right time

The Bombes – 221cm wide, 178cm high, moveable, with short legs on castors – were built by the British Tabulating Machine Co. at Letchworth. They were the ideal choice. In peacetime they had made Hollerith machines, office sorters and punched-card indexes in which relays were employed for recognizing and adding purposes. Harold (Doc) Keen, the Manager, was quick to grasp these very unusual requirements.[4]

## 'Prof' Turing

Alan Turing is one name many people associate with Bletchley Park. His tragic suicide in 1954, not yet forty-two, aroused a great deal of interest and sympathy. A play, a television film and a very thorough, sympathetic biography[5] have resulted, and he has become something of a cult figure.

The biography reveals an inadequate personality undergoing a wretched childhood, with parents abroad and having the singular misfortune to be sent to a particularly stuffy, backward public school where his outstanding talents were not even recognized, let alone appreciated. This school, Sherborne, even in the 1920s, still harboured a pre-Victorian distaste for science and the 'utilitarians', notwithstanding that these were the sources of the country's greatness and prosperity. With its rigid code, demanding absolute conformity, the school simply could not grasp that they had a quite outstanding mathematician in their midst, even when 'he spends a good deal of time apparently in investigations in advanced mathematics to the neglect of elementary work.'[6] If he appeared somewhat wayward – a scruffy, ink-stained, nail-biting, rather solitary fellow – then that is the mildly eccentric way the world expects its geniuses to be. But he did not 'fit'. Physically awkward, often without friends, not liked by masters, with a shy, hesitant manner and a high-pitched voice, he was going to be the perfect target, the hen in the public school yard that is pecked by the others. But he bore it all fairly stoically, always his own man, determinedly going his own way, trying to avoid, but not confront, the 'system'. He was interested in maths and science subjects, usually ignoring the rest – except in French, where the master, irritated by his indifference in class, was galled when he came top in the exam. Typically again, he was an absolute 'duffer' on the games field – the key activity in many public schools of the period – a mixture of natural clumsiness and complete indifference sealing his fate. Once again, very typically, he did well at cross-country running, a tallish, well-built youth doing his own, solitary thing.

After being threatened with expulsion, he was finally acknowledged, under a new headmaster as 'the sixth form maths genius' and became

48

a most unusual prefect. He then won a mathematics scholarship to King's College, Cambridge – as it happens the home of many code-breakers – which recognized his outstanding mathematical ability by making him a Research Fellow after graduation.

Two years later, in 1936, before going to Princeton University, in America, where he gained his doctorate, Turing published a paper, 'Computable Numbers', in which he suggested a mechanism that could move to the right or to the left a continuous tape marked in squares that could either read and change, or read and leave unchanged, the 0 or the 1 in each square. This will be familiar to those acquainted with computer basics. Turing showed that his projected machine could indeed calculate anything that was calculable. His paper created a considerable stir in some mathematical quarters. Later called by math-ematicians 'the universal Turing machine', it laid the theoretical basis for the modern general-purpose electronic computer which was eventu-ally developed after the War, and Turing has been acknowledged as the 'father of the computer'.

The Bombe he designed at BP, of course, was not of that order of complexity, but in keeping with the technology of the time. It was an electro-mechanical 'scanning and recognising' machine, automating what had previously been done by hand, and relied on relays. Neither was it at all 'general purpose', being designed very specifically as an aid to deciphering, and requiring an accurate crib.

At Bletchley, where he was known by his nickname, 'Prof', Turing was held in a certain awe, even wonder, by those who knew him. In a place where eccentricity, especially of the academic variety, was not at all unusual, Turing was an eccentric. Picking at the skin around his fingernails until they bled, wearing a variety of scruffy clothes, given to stammering, or being silent for long periods, avoiding eye-contact and sidling along sideways, he was accorded the good-natured tolerance granted to eccentric geniuses. This is how he would have been seen, and is remembered, by many. However, his general manner and behaviour suggest that he might have suffered from a mild degree of autism.

## Notes

1. A former pupil of Welchman's and probably the only girlfriend Turing ever had.
2. Hinsley and Stripp, *Codebreakers*, pp. 113–15.

3. Hodges, A., *Alan Turing: The Enigma* (London, Vintage, 1992), p. 183.
4. The only full description of the British Bombe is by Gordon Welchman in his book *The Hut Six Story* where one may also find an account of his diagonal board.
5. Hodges, *Alan Turing: The Enigma*.
6. Ibid., p. 26.

# Chapter 6

# HUT THREE – GETTING TO KNOW THE ENEMY

'Nothing, indeed, seemed less likely to house great matters than the ramshackle wooden building to which I reported in February, 1941' – Ralph Bennett[1]

Next to Hut Six was Hut Three – so close that bundles of papers were passed between them. The object of Hut Three, occupied by intelligence officers, was to make sense of the deciphered material that came out of Hut Six and somehow turn it all into comprehensible and useful despatches to be teleprinted to London or signalled to commanders in the field. For comprehensible it was not. The problem for Hut Three at the outset was the fragmentary nature, the sheer scrappiness, of the information arriving, and how to understand it. Peter Calvocoressi, himself a wartime head of Hut Three Air Section, has this to say, 'In intelligence . . . the beginning of wisdom lay in categorising and recording thousands of snippets of information which, although not unintelligible, since they have been rendered into German and thence into English, were nevertheless, largely pointless.'[2] These scraps could only be 'assembled, ordered and understood' if the officer had already gained considerable experience, or at the very least could refer to previously acquired information to see if this little piece of the jig-saw could be fitted in. In 1940, unfortunately, no store of carefully garnered information about the enemy, let alone intelligence officers capable of using it, were yet available. Then, early in 1941, came the 'Index', and the Air Index became, the central repository of what [we] knew about the Luftwaffe. Its importance cannot be exaggerated. It consisted of about two dozen girls and hundreds of thousands of cards. Every individual mentioned in Ultra had a card, every unit, every place . . . Then there were cards for pieces of equipment, for cover names, words or phrases which meant nothing at the time but might recur . . . the list was endless.[3]

## The 'bible' in red chalk

A copy of every message was given to the person in charge of the indexing shift. All words and phrases to be indexed were marked in red chalk. The girls, who included a fair number of university graduates, made up the cards by hand in ink. As Calvocoressi says, 'Like so much intelligence this work could be exceedingly tedious but it called for constant and thoughtful application.'[4] If one is inclined to wonder why graduates were necessary, or how the non-graduates managed, part of the answer is that Bletchley, in its initial euphoria, may have recruited too many people of unnecessarily high intellectual calibre.[5] The other part of the answer, unspoken though strongly implied, was that people of 'good background' would be less liable to betray secrets. Similar 'reasoning' partly applied to the Wrens who operated the Bombes, many of whom were educated to school certificate standard, but unlike Oxbridge recruits, were liable to police security checks.

The uses to which the Index could be put were never ending. 'What sort of a gadget goes by the name of PX7Q? How many serviceable aircraft were on Foggio airfield the day before yesterday? Do you know how much damage was done by Monday's raid on such-and-such target?'[6] The Index cards, about nine inches by five, began life in shoe boxes and ended up in purpose-made stands covering a long room. They were to grow to such an extent and become so vital to the work of Hut Three, and indeed, to the war effort as a whole that, according to one story, they were several times photographed (probably on micro-film), the copies being placed in a bomb-proof haven below the Bodleian Library in Oxford.[7] The heart of Hut Three, like that of Hut Six, was the Watch. In this case it comprised about six intelligence officers, mainly civilians, sitting around a table presided over by the head of the Watch. The messages arriving from Hut Six,[8] had, on one side of the paper, the original ciphertext (as intercepted), and on the other, the decipherment, now in German, but still in five-letter groups as required by Enigma procedure, so that the first job of the Watchkeeper was to divide the groups with pencil strokes into German words. On account of wireless reception conditions, not to mention fading and frequency drift, there were usually a number of corrupt words or even whole sentences that needed correction or gaps that needed to be filled. Although all the Watchkeepers had very fluent German this called for rather special skill.

Having knocked it into shape, the Watchkeeper would then translate it into English; his experience of military jargon, pro-formas, technical terms, even nicknames, usually carried him through, although specialist assistance, e.g. with technical terms or pro-formas, was available. Normally the member of the Watch would be familiar with the type of traffic dealt with in that particular key and on the particular wireless network that had been intercepted. He would then attach his English translation to the deciphered German text and hand it to the Head of the Watch for scrutiny. It was then passed to one of the Air or Military Advisers who shared a table nearby. Members of the Watch were expected to keep themselves fully informed by reading the translations of colleagues, even those of the other two Watches.

The Advisers,[9] after a spell in the Watch, had to know the intelligence situation thoroughly, their work falling into three parts. First, they had to evaluate the messages coming from the Watch. This was a heavy responsibility, having to keep in their minds the large overall picture of the military or air situation, yet at the same time be thoroughly familiar with large numbers of often quite small, detailed facts, the pieces of the jig-saw, or at least know in which part of the Index they might be found. Their evaluation, or interpretation, involved always being on the lookout for any new information, and to assess the importance of any newly disclosed detail however slight it might first appear.

A large part of the business of intelligence was to be in possession of associated facts, recent or remote, and to be skilled in making the correct associations. (Example: a message about the movements of '65 Army Corps IG' is transformed if you happen to know that this officer is Obersturmbannführer Dr Hoehne, the commander of the SS Wehrgeologen battalion which is engaged in the seismographic plotting of rocket missiles.)[10]

After evaluating the translated message the Adviser would add any comment he thought necessary, and in a case such as this would include a comment – in brackets preceded by the word 'comment' – which might include relevant information about Dr Hoehne, such as last-known location, his battalion's previous movements, special equipment used, all of which would derive from the Adviser's own knowledge, discussion with colleagues, and of course, searches of the Index. The usual reason given for the additional information was that in the first place it saved the recipients having to do the work all over again. A deeper reason may have been the opinion of the Admiralty's Room 40 in the First World War, and GC&CS's predecessor, that releasing 'raw' decoded messages invariably led to mistaken assessment by the recipients. In any case it caused resentment in the Whitehall intelligence 'community' and to this we will refer later.

## Secrets sent abroad

These recipients were: SIS headquarters in London (from where a selection of the day's teleprints was sent to the Prime Minister); the intelligence divisions of the War Office and Air Ministry; operational commands overseas. To London the most important material was sent in full by teleprinter, the rest in typewritten form 'by bag', i.e. by motorcycle despatch rider, once or twice a week. This would be background material, invaluable for intelligence staff. Everything that passed through the Watch was sent to London but not everything was sent to commands overseas. In fact, the Adviser had to decide whether information should be signalled to commands, to which command it should be sent and how quickly. If he had so decided, the Adviser would then have to draft the signal. In doing so he would summarize from one or more translated messages, being very careful to omit nothing of value. A main guiding principle in deciding whether to signal commands overseas was the 'need to know', i.e. not would it be of great interest but would it be of actual operational value. Priority was determined by the letter 'Z' ranging from one to five (ZZZZZ), the last being used sparingly. He would then pass all his papers to the Duty Officer for final scrutiny.

## The Duty Officer

Ralph Bennett, one of four Hut Three Duty Officers who had to give final authority to, and take responsibility for, everything released by

Hut Three, is concerned to show that the summarized version of the full teleprint that went to commands overseas, although never omitting vital operational intelligence, gives an incomplete picture of what went into these signals. Thousands of these wartime summaries may be seen in the Public Record Office, but, says Bennett, they give no more than

> a hint of the considerable intelligence servicing which almost every decode needed and received. The full meaning of the information conveyed by a message was only rarely self-evident from the translation alone, and it was usually necessary to draw out its significance by providing it with a context and setting it against a background as like as possible to that which would have been in the minds of the German sender and receiver.[11]

He goes on to say that with the help of Hut Three's indexes this could usually be done, in the teleprint, in considerable detail. Of course, the terms, 'evaluation', 'appreciation' and the like often used for this process, are simply euphemisms to avoid the word 'explanation', which may have given offence in some quarters.

The Duty Officer, who sat in a tiny office separated from the busy Watch Room, had to have an overall knowledge of the general war situation. His was 'a twofold responsibility, first to see that translation and signal [to field commanders] both faithfully represented the sense of the original . . . and asking [the Advisers] for appropriate changes if necessary.'[12] and then to ensure the security of the signals;[13] to see that nothing went out which might reveal the source; whether the recipient 'needed to know'; and if particular sections (which often co-operated), e.g. of intelligence divisions in London, needed to be informed, it should be on an all-or-none basis, so that they might consult together on an equal footing.

In their careful scrutiny of all the signals that passed through their hands the Duty Officers would never forget, not for a moment, that Ultra intelligence was based on messages, deciphered at BP, consisting of what the enemy was saying to himself and about himself, and BP often saw the War as the enemy would have seen it. All comments, therefore, however helpful, even vital, had to be clearly separated from the original content: corrupt texts, for example, however well restored by the Watch, had to be treated by the Advisers as doubtful, and qualified with agreed phrases such as 'strong' (fair, slight) 'indications'. A message intercepted without signature but positively attributable to a particular unit by, say, its call sign, was not allowed to be identified as, 'Fliegerkorps II reports' but as an 'unidentified unit (fair indications Fliegerkorps II) reports'. The Duty Officer bore a heavy responsibility. As he had initialled all signals his head was on the block. 'And he was the target for every kind of telephone call, sweet or sour, from chiefs of intelligence, chiefs of staff, the Chief of the Secret Service or the Prime Minister. For this job a certain temperament was required as well as a great deal of knowledge.'[14]

After the production line comprising the Watch, the Advisers and the Index, often hectically busy, especially if Hut Six, next door, happened to break two keys at the same time, let us turn to the 'back rooms' where equally thoroughgoing procedures were carried out, but at a less hectic pace.

Most immediately helpful to the Watchkeepers and Advisers was a language expert, Trevor Jones, who kept a well-thumbed index of technical terms used in the German forces, and was constantly amending it. This was particularly important in elucidating supply returns with their long German words for military spare parts and working out the meaning of abbreviations. These latter, the enemy may have considered, would both save Enigma time and act as a security check, but they did not reckon with Mr Jones!

## Military jig-saws

Then there was a section which undertook research into seemingly unfathomable problems. Knowledge of the enemy's armament could be crucial to Allied commanders, and one way Bletchley might obtain this information was by studying messages containing supply returns. These listed the numbers of tanks, guns, vehicles, ammunition, etc.; how many serviceable, how many under repair. But these were given according to a pro-forma with numbered items or paragraphs, e.g. 88mm guns might be listed as No. 22 with no further description. Some of these lists would yield under the close scrutiny of a skilled intelligence officer – others would not. By piecing together tiny scraps of evidence, and making reasonable inferences, the key would usually be found. Another expert, F.L. Lucas, dealt with general problems of intelligence. The Military Section, 3M, paralleled that of 3A, but we have dwelt on the (much larger) Air Section largely because the consistent breaking of the main Luftwaffe (Red) key provided Huts Six and Three with an almost unending flow of work. German Army Enigma was tougher than that of the Air Force. After the Fall of France in 1940 the German Army relied on their internal land lines until the invasion of southern Europe and North Africa in 1941. In any case, the German Army Enigma operators were more disciplined in their procedures than those of the Air Force which had expanded very rapidly indeed since its formation in 1935, and had recruited a poorer calibre of signaller.

Of course, the flow of Luftwaffe intelligence would contain items of military interest or inferences which could be drawn, but 3M did not have to be content with small fry. Blitzkrieg methods relied heavily on very close army–air force co-operation. For this purpose a *Fliegerverbindungsoffizier* – air liaison officer (often shortened to 'Flivo') – was attached to a Panzer division or corps. This officer, very properly, but to Bletchley most considerately, sent back to his air HQ detailed reports of army strengths, movements and intentions, but using his Enigma and wireless link – the Red key – which Hut Six often broke early in the day. This must partly have offset the lack of other military intelligence which did not arrive until deciphering began in the autumn of 1941.

The foregoing picture, a veritable powerhouse of intelligence gathering, processing and dissemination, where signals were often processed from interception to recipient in three to four hours, probably describes the two huts early in 1942, when the organization had fallen into a pattern that remained unchanged until the end of the war. Meanwhile, in the spring of 1941, the volume of signal intelligence and its importance had increased, with the Watch, the Advisers and the Index working a three-shift system. GC&CS were proving themselves the one sound, authentic source of information about the enemy when all else had failed.

## Creative anarchy

Despite their own dismal record since the outbreak of war, the service intelligence directorates were resentful in the first place, of GC&CS continuing to distribute the results of code-breaking. But, 'It turned out to be impossible for a single section to extract for each of the three services what was significant in a daily flow of thousands of signals of many different kinds.'[15] In fact, several groups at BP had already established direct links with various branches of the directorates in Whitehall, and as the Official History says, 'it was providing the serving officers of the directorates with their first close acquaintance with a body of men and women that must to them have seemed extraordinary for its lack of uniformity in outlook, organisation and procedure.'[16] Not only were the people disconcerting, but, 'GC&CS remained a loose collection of groups rather than forming a single, tidy organisation.'[16] Although this only reflected its pre-war history and its rapid growth since the start of the War (four-fold increase in size in sixteen months), 'the growth in its size and in the complexity of its activities had outstripped the experience of those who administered it.'[16] No one had planned it: like Topsy, it had 'just growed'. Not only was the organization, or rather lack of it, reprehensible in military eyes, even more so were the people who worked in it.

They were drawn from a section of society loosely called 'intellectuals', not a group particularly favoured by the military. I recall being told by a man who had just graduated before doing his National Service in the early 1950s, of being addressed by the officer-in-charge as follows: 'I understand a number of you are university people, I should keep rather quiet about it if I were you. There are those who say intelligence has no place in the army. I would say that is rather an extreme view, although I do think too much intelligence is rather vulgar.' There were certainly lots of academics at Bletchley, ranging from well-known professors to bright undergraduates (and even selected sixth-formers), the close proximity of Oxford and Cambridge ensuring that these (particularly Cambridge) were well represented, but the recruiting net for the 'best brains' had been cast widely, and Milner-Barry, head of the Hut Six Watch and a former British Chess Master, recalls making a 'profitable foray' to the Scottish Universities. The recruiting 'bag' included people from the museums, writers, barristers, actors, bank clerks, antiquarian booksellers. 'It would be invidious to put the various professions in any order of usefulness but teaching was certainly one of the best contributors'[17] wrote Bill Millward, Calvocoressi's deputy in Hut Three. He was probably thinking particularly of the 'translation Watch'. These were the sort of people who 'inaugurated and manned the various cells which had sprung up within or alongside the original sections. They contributed by their variety and individuality to the lack of uniformity. There is also no doubt they thrived on it, as they did on the absence at [BP] of any emphasis on rank or insistence on hierarchy.'[18] It was all new, strange and quite unprecedented. The military found it not only repugnant, but confusing. As the Official History

58

points out, they found it hard to distinguish between, on the one hand, a stronger central administration with whom they would have to negotiate about problems that would arise, and, 'on the other hand, the value of accepting and preserving the condition of creative anarchy, within and between the sections, that distinguished GC&CS's day-to-day work and brought to the front the best among its unorthodox and 'undisciplined' war-time staff.'[19] Creative anarchy, of course, was a prescription which was total anathema to service doctrine and tradition.

## 'No good, not even for intelligence'

Peter Calvocoressi, who, as mentioned earlier, became Head of Hut Three Air Section, has an instructive tale to tell about the attitude of the War Office in 1940. He decided to volunteer for the Army instead of waiting to be called up. Now Calvocoressi had an unusual background. Of Greek descent, he was born in British India and therefore a British subject by birth, his father being a naturalized British subject. He was an exemplary scholar and had been to the 'very best' places, winning a scholarship to Eton and then obtaining a first-class honours degree from Balliol College, Oxford. He had a flair for languages including German. He spent a day at the War Office where he went from one room to another being interviewed and undergoing tests. Finally, he 'arrived in an office where the accumulated results of the day's experiences lay tabulated on a sheet of paper with, at the foot, a verdict. Although from where I was sitting it was upside down, I could read it clearly enough. It ran: "No good, not even for intelligence".'[20] Calvocoressi put it down to the fact that he had cracked his head in a motor accident a few years earlier. But neither that nor any other consideration deterred the RAF who interviewed him and commissioned him as an intelligence officer within a week. From there the Bletchley 'trawl' caught up with him some months later.

GC&CS's problem was aggravated, 'because the monopoly of the directorates in the interpretation of [signal intelligence] was being threatened. The staff at GC&CS, recognising no frontiers in research, no division of labour in intelligence work, invaded the field of appreciation.' (i.e. evaluating Enigma messages and applying intelligence servicing) There's the rub. Although the Whitehall directorates saw this as an outrageous invasion of their territory, they 'were nevertheless ill-equipped and untrained'[21] to carry out the necessary research work. The reaction of the military bureaucrat would be, 'if you can't beat it, take it over' and there followed a series of running battles for the control of BP, which lasted until early 1942. (See Appendix 4 – Bletchley in Danger – for details of the attempted military 'take-over' in the autumn of 1941). Apart from the official administration, in the manor house, there were elements of hierarchy and rank at BP, but it was usually based on the nature of the work and the degree of responsibility carried. The main reason for the relaxed atmosphere was that, for the first year or two, certainly, the boffins and their immediate assistants were mostly the same sort of people, drawn from the middle and upper middle-class professional classes, the men often public school, and university, the women well-educated, often university graduates. This in itself would disconcert inquirers from the Whitehall intelligence directorates, who would have no idea of the status of the well-informed, well-spoken, person at the other end of the line. As Peter Calvocoressi said, 'There were Chiefs and Indians,' (at BP) 'but the Chiefs were not a different kind of person in the way that in the armed services, officers were officers and men were men.'[22]

## 'The best period of our lives'

Early in 1942, Edward Thomas, one of a small group of naval officers, arrived at BP.

> We naval newcomers were at once impressed by the easy relations and lack of friction between those in, and out of, uniform. Despite the high tension of much of the work, a spirit of relaxation prevailed. Anyone of whatever rank or degree could approach anyone else, however venerable, with any idea or suggestion, however crazy. This was partly because those in uniform had mostly been selected from the same walks of life as the civilians ... and partly because these were the people who saw most clearly what stood to be lost by a Hitler victory. All at the Park were determined to give their all to see this did not happen. Service Officers served gladly under civilians, and vice versa. Dons from Oxford and Cambridge worked smoothly together.[23]

But other impressions were not so pleasant. 'I vividly remember the sense of shock produced on my first arrival at the Park by the grimness of its barbed-wire defences, by the cold and dinginess of its hutted accommodation . . . But this was soon swept aside by the much greater shock of discovering the miracles that were being wrought at the Park.'[24]

In Hut Six the great majority of staff were aged under thirty, a goodly proportion under twenty-five; in Hut Three they were somewhat older. But they lived in a closed society and it was not easy to make social contacts outside. Their lives were almost confined to the sections in which they worked. One man could still regret, fifty years on, that a chance meeting in the BP canteen with 'a most attractive girl' could not be followed up as he never saw her again. The shift system, the rapidly growing population, the secrecy rules, all militated against chance liaisons. Nevertheless, there were many marriages. Derek Taunt was one of the lucky ones. 'It seemed to me that Hut Six formed a sufficiently large and varied propulation to provide congenial company for all. Perhaps I was biased, being of the male minority in a community where the women were exceptionally intelligent and attractive.'[25] Despite the shift system, and that only applied to 'key' sections, there were organized entertainments and games.[26] There was also the Home Guard from which not even senior boffins were exempt. Reg Parker, of Hut Six, was well known as a producer of revues; his wife Kathy was the Secretary of the BP Social Committee. More serious productions included a dramatization of *Pride and Prejudice*; those with a taste for classical music had visits from a string quartet and from the well-known wartime pianist, Myra Hess, and performances by talented BP members, such as Janet Milne who accompanied Mary Penny in Franck's violin sonata.

Gordon Welchman's recollections of life at Bletchley are worth mentioning. He recalls that it could be hard on shift workers; both on those billeted as well as on their landladies and their families – it was a problem of disturbed sleep. As a place of work, however, Bletchley was 'at least in pleasant rural surroundings', which, 'combined with the pleasant atmosphere of the whole place, contributed to our overall well-being.' He remembers much musical activity (especially because his wife was a singer and pianist), including a performance of Purcell's opera, *Dido and Aeneas*, and that the musical people joined forces with the theatrical group in at least two highly successful revues. He also mentions 'extensively-used hard tennis courts – the best players giving lunch-hour exhibition games'. He recalls the Hut Six Dance Committee who put on three or four dances a year – one on the eve of D-Day (it could not be cancelled because the date, known only to the very few, would then be guessed by the very many). 'Many of us look back to our Bletchley Park Days as the best period of our lives.'[27]

One of the Americans at Bletchley, Captain Bill Bundy, who later became a US Assistant Secretary of State, could not speak too highly of his time at BP. He remembers Hut Six as a 'terrific human experience' which he had not matched elsewhere. He ascribes this to the remarkable dedication and wonderful team spirit he found there.

Apart from the boffins and their immediate assistants, there were considerable numbers of support staff; clerks, typists, signallers, teleprinter operators, ('tele-princesses') electricians, service engineers. Some of these would be in uniform, some not. To feed the growing multitude there was a canteen used by most staff, whatever their service rank or civilian grade.[28] Academic influence was evident here too in the shape of a 'healthy food' diet affecting the menu. Large, rectangular dishes of raw carrot, turnip, beetroot and parsnip were usually on offer, as well as the staple wartime fare. Staff were brought to the Park by bus – often an ancient motor-coach – from where they were billeted, which could be as much as twenty miles away, the canteen break being the main opportunity to meet people other than their immediate colleagues.

## Notes

1. Hinsley and Stripp, *Codebreakers*, p. 30.
2. Calvocoressi, P., *Top Secret Ultra* (London, Cassell, 1980), p. 10.
3. Ibid., p. 61.
4. Ibid., p. 62
5. Welchman mentions the 'sheer piracy' they employed in their recruiting until, in the spring of 1941, a government body under C.P. Snow began to allocate scientific manpower.
6. Calvocoressi, P., *Top Secret Ultra*, p. 62.
7. The Index was set up in the spring of 1941 by Squadron Leader Cullingham (known as 'Cully'). He had previously worked on *Kelly's Directory*, and was absolutely the right man in the right job!
8. In the early stages papers were passed between the huts by a contrivance consisting of a tray, a broomhandle and string, the broomhandle to give audible warning. Opposing hatches had been cut in the adjoining walls.
9. The Air Advisers were RAF officers, later joined by two or three from the USAAF. They, together with the head, deputy and the Air Index, comprised the Air Section, (3A).

10. Calvocoressi, *Top Secret Ultra*, p. 11.
11. Bennett, R., *Ultra in the West: The Normandy Campaign of 1944–45* (London, Hamish Hamilton, 1979), p. 26.
12. Ibid., p. 29.
13. At the overseas commands the security of BP's signals was in the hands of SSUs (Special Signals Units); after August 1941, RAF personnel were attached to every command which was 'cleared' to receive Ultra intelligence. The actual wireless reception of the signals was by army Special Communications Units (SCU's). (See also p. 78.)
14. Calvocoressi, *Top Secret Ultra*, p. 61.
15. Official History, Vol. 1, p. 272.
16. Ibid., p. 273.
17. Hinsley and Stripp, *Codebreakers*, p. 26.
18. Official History, Vol. 1, p. 273.
19. Ibid., pp. 273–4.
20. Calvocoressi, *Top Secret Ultra*, p. 8.
21. Official History, Vol. 1, p. 274.
22. Calvocoressi, *Top Secret Ultra*, p. 10.
23. Hinsley and Stripp, *Codebreakers*, p. 45.
24. Ibid., p. 42.
25. Ibid., p. 109.
26. Other recreational facilities included: a library, radio and newspapers, a quiet room, bridge, chess, badminton and fencing. There was of course a beer hut.
27. Welchman, *The Hut Six Story*, p. 187.
28. As the Foreign Office was the official employer, most civilian staff were on its payroll, and carefully graded according to its archaic system. A female code-breaker, for example, might be graded 'linguist' whether she had any languages or not, as the 'nearest' 'appropriate' grade for a temporary civil servant, at £3–4 a week. For comparison, women in war-time aircraft factories could be paid £5 per week.

# Chapter 7

# HUTS FOUR AND EIGHT – SEARCHING FOR U-BOATS

The Translation Watch in Hut Four dealt with deciphered messages arriving from Hut Eight, who had the unenviable task of deciphering German naval Enigma. It was called the 'Z Watch', and started work around May 1941, after the various captures in the spring of that year had enabled Hut Eight to get going. After the messages had been finally deciphered using British Type-X machines, modified to simulate the Enigma, they were sent across to Hut Four where they were sorted by the No. 2 of the Watch, who had the responsibility of deciding which of these German texts – still in original letter groups and still containing many abbreviations and probably distortions – were of immediate concern to the Admiralty. These priority messages were given to No. 3 who would write out the message in the best German he could muster – abbreviations, technical terms, transmission corruptions and arcane naval jargon notwithstanding – and then pass it to No. 1, who would check it, translate it into English, allocate a number and decide whether to pass it for teleprinting to the Admiralty. Several copies were made for internal use. As in Hut Three, specialist groups (Naval Section VI provided back-up reference) were on hand to assist with new or unusual technical or naval terms, e.g. a new torpedo, and one group (in NSVI) produced a German-English dictionary of naval terms. A big headache for the translators was in expanding the abbreviations. The numbers allocated by No.1 would all be prefixed 'Z' (hence the 'Z Watch'). Those teleprinted, the most important, were prefixed 'ZTP', those translated from German (most of them), 'ZTPG'. Intelligence resulting from deciphering was often referred to as 'Z' information, or evidence. Thus, deciphered naval messages, once properly translated, went straight to the Admiralty and nowhere else. They were despatched without any intelligence evaluation or processing by intelligence officers of Hut Four. This, as we have seen, was quite unlike the procedure in Hut Three where Military and Air Advisers, backed up eventually by considerable resources, showed the Whitehall ministries and intelligence directorates just how good academics and others could be at the intelligence game. This going direct to the Admiralty contravened the old Room 40 precept that if you sent 'raw' intelligence – i.e. not evaluated and explained – the recipients were likely to misunderstand it. Of course, the Admiralty could say, with regard for example, to U-boat activity, 'we know where our ships are, we know where the convoys are, all you have to do is decipher the enemy signals, translate them into English and send them to us, we'll do the rest.' There is a reference in Kahn, *Seizing the Enigma* to the effect that during the Spanish Civil War, GC&CS had deciphered a message to two Italian submarines in the service of General Franco. The message appeared to say that ships breaking the blockade were to be sunk outside Spanish waters! This was barely credible, and it transpired that the GC&CS officer had placed his own entirely erroneous interpretation on an unclear text. It was a major gaffe, and the Admiralty are said to have ruled that in future deciphered messages come straight to us. In any case, the senior service, to begin with, had little faith in Bletchley's code-breaking, did not seem to grasp the importance of wireless traffic analysis (although they had acquired staff for the purpose), and had it not been for some early success with hand ciphers, might have washed their hands of Bletchley Park and regained code-breaking for themselves.

Christopher Morris, who worked on naval hand ciphers in Hut Four, well remembers attempts to counter official pessimism:

the first feather the Naval Section could put in its own cap . . . was the virtually self-evident '*Flugmeldesignal*' reporting enemy aircraft [i.e. enemies of the Germans], and enabling us to work out the German 'grid'. Naval officers were said to be impressed by the ability of German Naval Section to say that FLG meant '*Flugzeug*' (aeroplane) or that SOT meant '*Südost*' (south-east). Even after these modest triumphs pessimism

65

continued to prevail. As late as the summer of 1940 I myself heard Commander Denniston, head of GC&CS, saying to the head of Naval Section, 'You know, the Germans don't mean you to read their stuff, and I don't suppose you ever will.'[1]

And this at a time when the Luftwaffe Red key was already being broken daily!

Auxiliaries and small craft of the *Kriegsmarine* (Navy) did not carry Enigma, but used one of the higher-grade naval hand ciphers, usually the Dockyard key (*Werftschlüssel* or WS), in which there was a good deal of traffic, and as mentioned later, a very good source of cribs. As large vessels could only signal to these small craft using WS (first broken in 1940, but regularly and currently from about March 1941),

> almost every German warship from the *Tirpitz* down to destroyers used it on occasion and thereby told us her whereabouts; . . . Above all, it was often possible to learn from WS that a new U-boat had been commissioned and was exercising in the Baltic. The same cipher could also tell us of the routeing of coastal convoys, of damage suffered by German shipping, of the movements of hospital ships and transports serving the German army on the Eastern Front, and not least the volume of east or west-bound traffic in the Baltic. More than half of the WS signals deciphered were thought worth teleprinting to the Admiralty.[2]

Another important hand cipher, *Schlüssel* H, called 'Merchant Navy' at BP, was broken early in the War and although not producing intelligence of any great moment, was of considerable value, early in 1940, in showing a sceptical Admiralty that Naval Section could do something – demonstrating that not all enemy wireless signals were inviolable.

Unlike the War Office and the Air Ministry, the Admiralty was not only an administrative, but an executive department, in direct command of its ships at sea. For example, at the time of the search for the *Bismarck*, Admiral Tovey, Commander-in-Chief of the Home Fleet, in the battleship *King George V*, was made to realize that his squadron was sailing in the wrong direction, having misinterpreted the bearings given to them!

Although the Admiralty, or to be precise, Naval Intelligence Division, insisted on their intelligence rations not being diluted by any civilian hand, this is not to say that the intelligence officers of Hut Four did not eventually build up a relationship with the officers of the OIC,[3] when the latter had learned to know and trust them. In the long eighteen-months gap before substantive intelligence from Enigma deciphering appeared, Hut Four made what offerings they could, in order, as it were, to justify their existence. 'We . . . recognised the three-letter German Naval Air Code . . . and did some rudimentary wireless telegraphy (W/T) traffic analysis.'[4] Sometimes, this produced startling results. Harry Hinsley (the late Professor Sir Harry Hinsley), then a young undergraduate recently recruited from Cambridge, used a direct line from Hut Four to the OIC which he actuated by turning a handle. The hardened sea-dogs at the other end must have wondered what some young civilian could possibly tell them about naval intelligence, which, in any case, was the OIC's business. Nor were they inclined to pay attention, 'until, some time before the invasion of Norway . . . (there were) indications from German wireless behaviour that something unusual was taking place in the Baltic.[5] Somewhat later, a few days before the aircraft-carrier, HMS *Glorious*, was sunk . . . they showed some interest in indications that heavy ships were about to leave the Baltic, but were not sufficiently convinced to send a warning to the Home Fleet.'[6]

## 'The Cardinal'

Looking back, Hinsley realized that it must have appeared as enormous presumption, 'and they were not to know that traffic analysis . . . was an academic exercise which, like the elucidation of a Latin text . . . called more for immersion in detail than for experience at sea. Except occasionally, moreover, it was not so sound a basis for reliable inferences as I no doubt believed it to be.'[7] But this was certainly one such occasion. Neither was the OIC too proud, small-minded or bureaucratic to pretend it did not happen, or to try and cover it up. On the contrary, they were in a serious situation and decided to cultivate the new 'source' – long hair, spectacles and all.

> It [OIC] immediately invited me to spend a month in the Admiralty [where he was dubbed 'the Cardinal' – after Cardinal Hinsley]. It sent me on the first of several visits to the Home Fleet at Scapa, where I stayed on board the flagship and walked the deck with Admiral Tovey and his staff. And on my return it did all in its power to ensure through the regular exchange

of visits, and with the assistance of new scrambler telephones, that there should be complete collaboration between the OIC and the Naval Section.[8]

Harry Hinsley never looked back and his career could serve as a model for what the War could occasionally do for able young men of humble origin. As suggested, Harry Hinsley and Hut Four were not overworked for the first eighteen months of the War. 'Until the spring of 1941 my share in the collaboration [with OIC] was still confined to the study of the external behaviour of the German Navy's wireless traffic,' which he 'undertook both for clues that might be of operational value to the OIC and in case it might give any help to the cryptanalysts [code-breakers] . . . I do not remember that it helped the Admiralty much.'[9] Nor, as he says, did it help the code-breakers. Nevertheless, the name 'Hinsley' continued to shine brightly in the naval firmament. 'That relations were close and harmonious, however, is evident from two Admiralty signals of this period [autumn, 1940]. The first is an enquiry from the Home Fleet: 'What is your source?' The second is the Admiralty's reply, of which the full text is: 'Hinsley'.[10]

In the following year another occasion arose for Hinsley to show that he was a better intelligence officer than his counterparts in OIC. After the lucky capture of cipher sheets from the wreck of the *Krebs* at the time of the Lofoten raid (March 1941), Hinsley, studying the newly deciphered material, found evidence 'that the Germans were keeping trawlers permanently on station to make weather reports from the Iceland-Greenland area – and led me to conclude that, although they were not using it for their signals,[11] the ships carried the Enigma.'[12] As a result, BP Naval Section were able to recommend the capture of one of these weatherships, and later, a second. In between came the chance but very fortunate capture of U-boat U-110, from which vital documents were obtained (see Chapter 11). As a result of these captures, both planned and accidental, Hut Eight was able to attack the problem of the naval Enigma. Hinsley continues, 'The fact that the problem was solved from that date [June 1941] so that the main naval key was thereafter read regularly for the rest of the war, was mainly due to the close relations that had been built up between Bletchley and the OIC.'[13]

To suggest that 'the problem was solved' was much too sweeping a statement, and Hinsley qualifies it as follows: 'Apart from a new key used by U-boats that was unreadable between February and December

1942, all important naval keys were read for the rest of the war.'[14] This retrospective gloss, not mentioned by Hinsley in the Official History, needs amplification. It was precisely during this period in 1942, when Bletchley fell silent, that the Allies were losing the war in the Atlantic, and therefore probably the War itself. The year 1942 was the 'annus horribilis' in which 1,160 vessels (over 6m tons) and many thousands of lives, were lost. When the 'U-boat key' was broken in December, deciphering was only continued with great difficulty, subject to many delays and interruptions, and could not prevent the Battle of the Atlantic reaching its climax in March 1943, when the enemy achieved his greatest success against the convoys, Britain's lifeline was threatened, food rations severely reduced, and the Admiralty in despair. The phenomenal reversal of fortune that followed in April and May owed something to deciphering but mostly to the Allies at last giving priority to the Atlantic and bringing to bear a whole arsenal of modern weapons against the U-boat.

Harry Hinsley's renown had spread beyond the confines of Bletchley Park and naval intelligence. In 1943 we find him, a 24-year-old undergraduate, crossing the Atlantic in a fast destroyer, on his way to Washington, there to help negotiate the 'Brusa' agreement with the US Government. The acronym, which stands for 'Britain-United States of America', was devised by him on his way across. The exchange of decoded information between the Allies had not been as willing, as full or as fast as it should have been, and the agreement provided for total exchange thereafter; German intelligence going to Washington, Japanese to BP. In February 1946 he attended a secret London conference which renewed in peacetime, under the governments of Attlee and Truman, the Brusa agreement for total exchange of information in what had become, or was very soon to become, the Cold War. Harry Hinsley was allowed to hold his engagement party at the same rather grand mansion in the west end of London where the conference had taken place. Although he provided a lot of the drink himself, as a Fellow of St John's College, Cambridge, he managed to get the College to provide some from its cellars. In fact Harry Hinsley, who had left Cambridge for BP at the end of his second year,[15] was elected a Fellow of St John's in 1944 without ever having taken his degree, and was able to command the wine-cellars before even taking up the appointment! Clearly, the establishment thought very highly of Harry and his college was proud of him. More honours and rewards were to follow. After his engagement in March,[16] he went to say goodbye to 'C' (Sir Stewart Menzies, head of the Secret Service and of BP) whom he therefore must have known quite well. There he was offered, and accepted, a gold watch, and was given some money to spend on his honeymoon. Later that year he was awarded the OBE, but as in the case of a few other Bletchleyites (i.e. the few who got anything at all), no higher award could be made lest it should draw attention to the secret nature of their war work. The citation would probably have read, or included, 'war service, HM Foreign Office, 1939-46'. Sir Harry went on to become Professor of the History of International Relations, Master of St John's College and Vice-Chancellor of Cambridge University. He was chief editor of the official *History of British Intelligence in the Second World War* (HMSO) five vols., 1979–90, and was knighted in 1985.

According to a former student of Hinsley's, Peter Linehan, writing an obituary in the *Independent* newspaper, his lectures were 'spellbinding', and even less than a year before he died, in February 1998, 'he kept an enormous post-prandial Cambridge audience on the edge of its collective seat while he reminisced on Bletchley days, without a note and for exactly the hour prescribed.' Linehan also mentions Hinsley's 'How I sank the *Bismarck*' (which was the undergraduates' title, not his, or not entirely his) being 'a regular show-stopper at Cambridge college history societies' (see also, Who sank the *Bismarck*? p. 111).

Altogether, there was something of 'le Bletchley, c'est moi' about Sir Harry.

In 1942 Alexander, Turing and Welchman were summoned to the Foreign Office, the official employer, and each presented with a cheque for £200; the explanation given that owing to the secret nature of the work no formal award could be expected. Nevertheless, after the War Turing and Welchman were awarded the OBE. In contrast, the leading US code-breaker, Colonel William Friedman, was awarded the Medal for Merit and the National Security Award.

The German naval Enigma was an extremely hard nut to crack. Although it employed the same machine as the Army and Air Force, the Navy used a thoroughgoing and complex procedure designed to defeat internal spies, external eavesdroppers, direction finders and code-breakers, and even took into account the possibility of the capture of several elements of the system.

Hut Eight's principal code-breakers at the outset, early in 1940, were Kendrick and Twinn, both of whom had been employed by GC&CS before the War, and Alan Turing, who had occasionally 'helped out' at weekends prior to the War. They were later joined by Hugh Alexander, another outstanding King's College, Cambridge mathematician, a British Chess Champion, and a capable organizer.

They soon began to realize the formidable nature of their problem. Chance captures of enemy vessels during 1940 enabled them, from documents recovered, to decipher about six days of the naval Home Waters key, and in June 1940, the Enigma procedure was recovered from U-boat U-13, the study of which must have been a sobering, not to say daunting, experience.

They learnt that only officers were allowed to set the wheels (three out of eight) and rings of the naval Enigma, and this was done every other day. The Enigma operator continued with a lengthy, complicated procedure, an abbreviated version of which is given in Appendix 3.

It shows that compared with the military (and air force) Enigma, there appeared to be nothing left to chance. Weak points like an operator frequently using say, his girlfriend's initials, or swear words, as randomly chosen indicators, are eliminated, as the naval indicators are chosen from a book, then crossed out, never to be used again. The possibility of the receiving operator misunderstanding the indicators is obviated by having them enciphered using a secret bigram table, with built-in safeguards. Further delights awaited them; the 'officer only' messages, doubly-enciphered; the Short Signal Book, first encoded before being enciphered; and finally the Short Weather Cipher, each item of a weather situation and area reduced to a single letter, first issued in the autumn of 1940. Meanwhile, as Hut Eight staff waited for their first break, which came with the series of enemy vessels captured in 1941, they worked on German railway ciphers.

Hut Eight was eventually divided into a linguistics section and a mathematical section. The former, known as the 'crib room', was headed by Shaun Wylie, who before becoming a mathematician had had a classical education. Early in 1941 he was recruited by Turing who had known him at Princeton (USA) where they both obtained their doctorates in mathematics. The mathematical section, in an adjoining room, struggled with naval messages which did not yield a crib. This was headed by Alan Turing as was the hut as a whole. There was a hatch connecting the two sections which collaborated closely and frequently.

The larger room, known as the 'big room', housed support staff, mostly young women, who were employed on a variety of tasks such as punching holes in Banbury sheets, using Hollerith equipment for sorting the enciphered traffic, keeping records, and testing Bombe results on modified Type-X machines.

The 'cribsters' would search, for example, weather reports, trying, in the spring of 1941, to establish beginnings of messages, addressees and senders. This was not unlike the preliminary work that had been done in Hut Six a year earlier. The crib room was something like an intelligence section in that an index of cribs, or potential cribs, could be built up and one success lead to another. The work called for linguistic skills such as the meticulous attention to small detail typical of classical scholars. Hilary Brett-Smith (later Lady Hinsley) had been an Oxford academic, teaching Anglo-Saxon, and was said to have been recruited because of the speed with which she could solve *The Times* crossword-puzzle.

The mathematical section, the 'Banburists', took the messages which could not, at first, be tested on the Bombes, although in practice, especially in August 1941, when the captured material ran out, and Hut Eight was severely tested (as Hut Six had been in May 1940), the two sections worked almost as one. 'There followed [after the beginning of August] an exciting period when almost every day was solved with varying delays, by a combination of Banburismus and cribs,'[17] recalls Rolf Noskwith, a recently recruited cribster.

'Banburismus [the name derives from Banbury where the sheets used in the technique were printed] was an elaboration of a method called the "clock method" by Rejewski . . . [it] depends largely on the indicating system (for the initial settings of the rotors [wheels] for individual messages.)'[18]

## Banburismus

Although relying on holes punched in paper sheets rather than on elaborate machinery, Banburismus, albeit labour and time consuming, acquitted itself well. Apart from sliding the sheets along and recording the results, which was slow and tedious, the technique involved a good deal of mathematics, including statistical analysis and probability. The following therefore, is an abbreviated outline.[19]

The technique depended on the naval indicator system, a brief description of which is given in Appendix 3. Assuming the British had somehow acquired the secret bigram tables which protected the indicators, perhaps by capture, the Banburists refined their techniques for finding which bigram table (out of a set of ten) was currently in use. They could then try to work their way back to the position the Enigma machine wheels were in when the sending clerk tapped out his three-letter message indicator from which the message setting, as shown in the machine's windows, was derived. The Banburismus method was employed first of all, to ascertain the relationship between the third letter of the trigraph and the true right-hand or fast wheel setting for the message.[20] The Banburists would compare pairs of enciphered messages – as they arrived from interception – where the three-letter groups (mentioned above) started with the same digraph of two letters, e.g. HYU and HYV. This was done by punching holes in the Banbury sheets which had lots of alphabets (A–Z) printed side by side – the longer the message the wider the sheet needed. The holes punched in the successive alphabets were the successive letters of a message, a job for the 'big room girls'. The punched sheets would be laid one above the other, on a dark-surfaced table, lining up the first alphabets, and were slowly moved, or staggered, so that at each stagger, some dark spots might appear where two punched holes – the same letter – coincided. Sequences of such spots corresponding to 'repeats' of one, two or three letters would be counted, converted into 'scores' and recorded. Repeats of four letters or more were found by putting all the traffic through Hollerith sorting equipment.

The 'scores' were in units of 'weights of evidence'; originally developed by Turing, later refined by Good, the 'ban' was a piece of evidence that might make a hypothesis ten times more likely than it might otherwise be. A piece of evidence would be expressed mathematically with its score. These pieces of evidence would be combined to determine the relationship between the third letter of the trigraph and the setting of the fast wheel. At the same time they would try to discover the position of the right-wheel notch. This was a small groove cut in the wheel's alphabet ring which engaged and moved on the middle wheel when 'turn-over point' was reached. After this point all the wheels might have moved and those pairs of messages expected to have repeats would not have them. Wheels I–V of the eight German naval wheels had their notches cut at Q-R, E-F, V-W, J-K, Z-A; if the middle wheel turned over between E-F it could be identified as wheel II.

In practical terms identifying the right wheel significantly reduced the number of possible wheel orders to be tested on the Bombes; from 336 to as few as forty-two. The 'players' found Banburismus utterly absorbing; far from easy yet not hard enough to produce a nervous breakdown!

## Notes

1. Hinsley and Stripp, *Codebreakers*, p. 237 (from *Intelligence & National Security*, Vol. 1, No. 1, Frank Cass & Co. Ltd, 1986).
2. Ibid., p. 236.
3. Operational Intelligence Centre.
4. Dakin in Hinsley and Stripp, *Codebreakers*, p. 52.
5. For example, sudden increase in wireless activity, movement of wireless networks, springing up of new ones.
6. F.H. Hinsley in Hinsley and Stripp, *Codebreakers*, p. 78.
7. Ibid.
8. Ibid.
9. Ibid.
10. Ibid., p. 79.
11. i.e. their routine weather reports (see Official History, Vol. 1, p. 337 and Appendix 12).
12. Hinsley and Stripp, *Codebreakers*, p. 79.
13. Ibid.
14. Ibid., p. 80. Some important keys were not read; for example, after the Allies invaded Europe (June 1944), the German Navy began to issue each U-boat with its own individual key. These were not broken at BP and would have required greatly increased resources to do so. Sinkings began to increase, although the overall total remained comparatively small.
15. With a First in Part I of the Historical Tripos.
16. To Hilary Brett-Smith, who had been a code-breaker at BP.
17. Hinsley and Stripp, *Codebreakers*, p. 119.
18. Good, ibid., p. 155.
19. For a fuller, but more technical account, see Good, ibid., pp. 155–8.
20. For operation of Enigma wheels see Appendix 1, p. 170.

# Chapter 8

# HOW NOT TO
# KEEP A SECRET

Producing Ultra intelligence is one thing; putting it into the hands of those able and willing to make use of it is another. Ultra was the best kind of military intelligence. The 'usual sources' all had their drawbacks: spies, interrogation of prisoners, aerial reconnaissance, resistance fighters, captured documents and equipment, all, to some degree, chancy, unreliable, slow. Ultra suffered none of these defects and possessed two enormous advantages. The best intelligence must be authentic and quick. Ultra was authentic because it came from enemy commanders talking to each other or reporting to their headquarters – in a word – eavesdropping. And it was usually fairly prompt, at its best inside three hours from interception to final signal. It has been argued that Ultra was at times insufficient, because some enemy communication was by land-line or courier, resulting in an incomplete intelligence picture. But as the War expanded south and east the enemy had to use wireless more and more, even for top-level communication (see Colossus, Chapter 13).

Uniquely, the British were often privy to the plans, resources and decisions of their enemies – the big question then was how would they make use of it all. Even when the picture happened to be incomplete, BP's resources – technical experts, language specialists, teams concentrating on enemy weapons, the German war economy, the German railways, the weather, and so on – became so great as to fill many of the gaps. And the intelligence officer's job was, to a large extent, filling gaps. So knowledgeable about the enemy did Bletchley become, that it was said if one wanted to find three people who knew most about the Luftwaffe, you would find them, not in Germany, but at Bletchley Park! But for all that, the problem remained of distributing these gems to those who needed them, and then of convincing the recipients that this intelligence was so authentic, so reliable, so trustworthy, that military dispositions could be made on the strength of it, and men's lives risked.

In January 1940, however, when intelligence deriving from deciphering Enigma messages first became available, the head of the Secret Service, in order to 'protect', as he would have seen it, his newly-found and potentially valuable 'source', decided to pretend it was something other that what it was. Translations of the early Enigma decipherments were disguised as Secret Service reports, from an agent, 'Boniface'. The Admiralty would have none of it – knew or guessed the true source and insisted that OIC be sent undisguised material straight from BP. But for military and air intelligence branches in Whitehall, the fiction was maintained. As was mentioned earlier, the SIS had a poor standing in Whitehall, being blamed, among other things, for providing the service directorates with much poor, or even misleading, information about Germany prior to the War.[1] Moreover, the true identity of Boniface intelligence was not revealed to those middle-ranking intelligence officers who actually drew up reports and briefings, and whose experience had made them sceptical about information from agents (especially SIS's agents). In fact, only a very small number of people were initially let into the secret, 'which, apart from the OIC, included the three Directors of Intelligence and, we must assume, the Chiefs of Staff and the War Cabinet'.[2] Worse, as the officers who 'drew up the briefings for the indoctrinated authorities' (those let into the secret) were themselves ignorant of the true source of Boniface, they made up their briefings from a variety of sources, and 'it does not appear that these authorities (i.e. those in the know) had any way of distinguishing the Enigma from the other ingredients that went into the briefings.'[3]

## A tangled web . . .

When the military and air advisers in Hut Three sent signals to 'commanders in the field', what happened in practice was that such signals would be received by the senior intelligence officer in the command who himself knew about Enigma-based intelligence, but, to begin with, when he briefed his commander-in-chief and chief of staff, was not allowed to mention the true source. Now, 'commanders in the field', like intelligence staffs in London, were very wary of 'agents' reports', or of a non-attributable source, no matter how authentic his intelligence officer declared it to be. This was asking the commander to take the intelligence officer's word, and some commanders did not think highly of the intelligence profession in general, or perhaps of this officer in particular. The result of such self-defeating procedures was that commanders probably gave too little weight to the intelligence, or just ignored it, not realizing its impeccable origins. Oh, what a tangled web we weave when first we practice to deceive!

By the spring of 1941 it was no longer possible to conceal from the intelligence staffs in Whitehall the true source of the many so-genuine-sounding messages that arrived. Indeed, to any alert intelligence officer, the steady flow of such messages could *only* have been based on decoding enemy signals – their very nature and content testifying daily to this assumption. A whole regiment of 'agents', embedded in the higher echelons of the German armed forces, could hardly have done as well.

In the autumn of 1940, Italy, which had entered the War when France was almost defeated, invaded Egypt on 15 September – the day the Battle of Britain ended – and at the end of October also attacked Greece which soon ended in complete failure. The British position in the Middle East began to look serious, especially if Nazi Germany should come to the aid of its Axis partner. In addition to these ominous events BP's deciphered messages now began to give information about German penetration of the Balkans.

As early as November 1940, it was decided that intelligence resulting from breaking the Luftwaffe Red key should be sent direct to Cairo, and Combined Bureau Middle East was set up, responsible for co-ordinating code-breaking in the three services. It is indicative of the precariousness of the times – Hitler's invasion of Britain (Operation Sealion) had only just been called off, British cities were being heavily bombed – that the War Office and Air Ministry should have permitted this oddball secret service organization, staffed mainly by civilians, to select, paraphrase and despatch secret operational intelligence (although they regretted it later – see Appendix 4). But that is what they did – or rather, what they intended to do – but for the difficulties that held up the establishment of this new service for some four months.

The obsession with the super-security of the 'Enigma secret' – that

Britain was listening to enemy wireless signals – was almost pathological. Although the 'secret' could no longer be concealed from the Whitehall directorates, great pains were taken to see that no Enigma items were included in any intelligence summaries these people might circulate widely. But when it came to commands overseas, 'Whitehall remained anxious to apply its own earlier and stricter rule by which knowledge of the source was withheld even from its immediate recipients,' and the new service 'was held up until arrangements which met this requirement had been negotiated and laid down'.[4]

Meanwhile, in the spring of 1941, Italian and German forces were in conflict with British troops in North Africa and in Greece, and the pressure of these events may have finally moved the holders of the rigid views as to the perfect security of the 'most secret source', the logical outcome of which is that it would be better to lose wars than lose the secret. In the event, it was not until mid-March that the security arrangements were finalized and signals began to be sent over a special RAF wireless link – the messages carrying the prefix OL (Orange Leonard). To begin with the signals were entrusted to the Director of the Combined Bureau personally, and he sent them to a very limited number of people at the three service intelligence headquarters. 'Though he suspected that it was the Enigma, he was not formally told this until the beginning of May.[5] Thereafter, he continued to withhold from the recipients any information as to its source: they were told only that it was "completely reliable"[6] and, 'though the HQs could take it into account in framing operational orders to lower commands, such use of the intelligence was permitted only when it could be made to seem that it had been disclosed by other sources like reconnaissance or low-grade signal intelligence.'[7] and the Official History concludes, in much understated officialese, that, 'these security precautions, however understandable, blunted the impact of the intelligence in Cairo and limited its usefulness to the Middle East Commands.'[8] By August 1941, after the disaster in Crete, the charade finally came to an end and 'Boniface', like Bunbury before him, could be safely killed off. Special Communications Units were set up to handle the transmission and reception of BP signals, with corresponding Special Liaison Units attached to each HQ 'cleared' to receive Enigma-based messages, and these units deciphered the signals, explained their full weight and significance, and ensured they were promptly returned and destroyed, so that they would not be seen by persons other than those intended, or, in the worst case, captured by the enemy.

The intelligence resulting from breaking Enigma messages was thereafter called 'Ultra', strictly, 'Most Secret Ultra'[9] its signals carrying the prefix CX/MSS.

## Notes

1. In fact, a good deal of information about Nazi Germany, its regime, economy, and war preparations, had been available from the European, especially the Swiss, and even the German, press and radio, if only these 'intelligence' directorates had kept an ear to the ground, but they had not.
2. Official History, Vol. 1, p. 138.
3. Ibid.
4. Ibid., Vol. 1, App. 13, p. 571.
5. The Director of CBME at Heliopolis, near Cairo, was Captain Freddie Jacob, the deputy head of the military section at BP who would have certainly known the true source.
6. Official History, Vol. 1, p. 571.
7. Ibid.
8. Ibid., pp. 571–2.
9. Later, under American influence, 'Top Secret Ultra'.

# Chapter 9

# GREECE AND CRETE –
# THE CODE-BREAKERS
# LEND A HAND

If Ultra intelligence could eventually help to win battles, its first excursion into the field of military action resulted in a less glamorous but still vital role: helping to prevent a defeat turning into a disaster.

By January 1941, the Italians in Libya had surrendered to British forces under Wavell, and in the following month the Germans under Rommel invaded Tripoli with the intention of reversing the Italian defeat and stiffening Italian resistance to the British.

At this crucial time Bletchley Park asserted its usefulness. Peter Calvocoressi, later to become head of the Hut Three Air Section, sums up this period well.

> Ultra came into its own in the first months of 1941 through the richness and promptitude of the information which it gave about the movements of stores, staffs, troops and aircraft into south-eastern Europe, . . . [and this] Luftwaffe Ultra was supplemented by regular breaks of transport or railway Enigma. These enabled us to follow practically day by day the German occupation of Rumania and then Bulgaria, pointing unequivocally to the invasion of Greece . . . It was in these months that confidence in Ultra was established, together with increasing expectations of it and reliance upon it.[1]

To add to their daily successes against the Luftwaffe general key (Red), BP broke a new Luftwaffe Mediterranean key (Light Blue) in

80

February. All of this was no doubt appreciated and perhaps admired, by the very small coteries in London and Cairo who were privy to deciphered Enigma intelligence. The problem was to get it into the hands of those who badly needed it. In these circumstances it must be rated as something of a bureaucratic miracle that the new direct wireless link to the Middle East which came into service in mid-March should be extended to British General Headquarters in Athens by 27 March. This was exactly ten days before the German invasions of both Yugoslavia and Greece, Belgrade being savagely bombed with large numbers of civilian casualties.

## Reducing the scale of the calamity

The British, not entirely trusted by the Greek Government, and themselves misinformed (Eden, the Foreign Secretary, sent a grossly over-optimistic estimate of the possibility of defending Greece), were persuaded to send troops. This was contrary to the advice of the Commander-in-Chief, Middle East, Wavell, who did not wish to see his North African force robbed of some of its best troops. Some 60,000 men, mostly Australian and New Zealand troops, were no match for far more numerous and better-armed German forces. General Wilson, commanding the British and Commonwealth force, could only retreat. In the difficult circumstances, Wilson's withdrawals were very well timed, and here credit must be given to the Enigma intelligence he and his commanders in forward headquarters were now receiving. The broken Luftwaffe keys yielded the vital element. Although German army Enigma had not yet been broken, the Luftwaffe liaison officers (the 'Flivos', BP's 'friends at Court') attached to the advancing army HQs, carefully supplied their own air headquarters (and, of course, the British) with exact details of the whereabouts, names and next moves of their units. This was the first time that commanders in the field had been told the true nature of the source and of its utter reliability. One line to which General Wilson had to withdraw was based on Olympus, but Enigma intelligence informed him, in time, that he was about to be outflanked. 'Enigma information that German armour intended to operate to the south of Olympus reached the GOC (Wilson) on 15 April and undoubtedly influenced his decision of that date to withdraw to Thermopylae – a decision of which it has been said by the Australian official historian that, "if the . . . withdrawal had begun a day later it would have been disastrous for the British force".[2]

After Greece came Crete. The evacuation from the Greek mainland was mainly successful, and had there not been an acute shortage of shipping; the bulk of the almost 51,000 men evacuated from the beaches would have been taken to Egypt; but without air cover, even the passage to Crete was perilous, the Luftwaffe sinking two destroyers and four troop transports, with heavy loss of life. Although some units went to Alexandria, about 35,000 British, Commonwealth and Greek troops had arrived in Crete by the beginning of May 1941. Most of their artillery, transport and signals equipment had been left behind, and to begin with, they were no longer a coherent force. Some British units, however, had been on the island since the previous November, and, heedless of orders from London, very little had been done by Middle East HQ to turn Crete into the bristling fortress which Churchill had envisaged.

Meanwhile, Enigma-based intelligence – so valuable in ensuring the orderly withdrawal from Greece – began to give clear indications of a planned airborne attack on a Mediterranean island. As early as 25 March 1941 it was revealed that the newly-formed Fliegerkorps XI, a parachute and airborne force under General Student, was assembling very large numbers of Ju 52 aircraft which were used for towing gliders. There was no reference in these messages to a particular target until a month later (26 April), when Operation Crete was specifically mentioned in a Luftwaffe Enigma message.[3]

It is symptomatic of the confusion still surrounding Enigma-based information at that time that the Official History can comment, 'Nor was he (the C-in-C Middle East) alone in suspecting that the Enigma references to Crete might be part of a German cover plan for a descent on Cyprus and Syria; on 30 April the Chiefs of Staff still harboured this suspicion.'[4] 'Confusion' is perhaps too charitable.

## A 'heaven-sent' opportunity

Deciphering the Luftwaffe Enigma continued to give a more and more detailed account of the preparations and movements of the airborne troops. 'And most important of all, on 6 May it vouchsafed nothing less than the German estimate of the probable date of the completion of their preparations – 17 May – and complete final operational orders for

1. Enigma cipher machine (with inner lid closed) as used by the German Army and Air Force in the Second World War. The plugboard is at the front, behind which is a German typewriter keyboard, to the rear of which is the lampboard.

2. The British Type-X cipher machine as supplied to the Army and RAF for high level communication in the Second World War. It was never 'broken' by the enemy.

3. Almost certainly Hut Six about 1942. The operators are using Type-X cipher machines modified to simulate German Enigma machines.

4. Intercept Control Room, Hut Six, Bletchley Park, 1943. From here the interception or listening stations were directed to receive those enemy wireless networks in whose transmitted messages the code-breakers were particularly interested.

5. The Turing-Welchman 'Bombe'; a high-speed, electro-mechanical machine used in the later stages of deciphering large numbers of enemy messages.

6. German military Enigma Machine with inner lid raised revealing the lamps and the wheels of the 'scrambler unit' with their independently adjustable wheel rings.

7. Wrens (WRNS - Women's Royal Naval Service) operating the 'Colossus' machine. This is probably the Mark II machine, the world's first electronic computer, and was used before and during the invasion of Europe in 1944.

STANDING L-R. S.M.A. Banister, Miss M. Bruce, Maj. W. Bundy, Mrs. Banister, Miss M. Ridley, Cpl. H. Thielbar, A. Coldwell, A.H. Read, Cpl. J. Fletcher, Miss H. McCreath, Lt. A. Levenson, Sgt. G. Evans, Miss A. Pegg, Sgt. A. Lewis, Sgt. J. Leahy, D. Nicoll, Miss B. Morgan (hidden), Miss P. Storey, Miss D. Hinton, Sgt. J. Hyman, Mrs J. Hyman, M. Chamberlain, Mrs R.H. Parker, Maj. D. Babbage, J. Evans, R.H. Parker, R. Brook, J. Hamilton, Miss L. Hermelin, A. Smith, Lt. W. Bijur, Miss B. Morris, Maj. J. Manisty, Miss N. Cropper.

SITTING L-R. Miss E. Hollington, Sgt. H. Porter, C.S. Williams, R. Pendred, Sgt. G. Hurley, Miss S. Castor, N. Forward, Mrs. H. Smith, Miss K.J. Jay.

8. Hut Six, Bletchley Park staff celebrating VE Day, 8 May 1945. These were the people concerned with registration, intercept control, crib-hunting and other stages of code-breaking.

the execution of the assault.' These orders were transmitted in unusually great detail.

> They listed the exact stages of the plan from D-day, beginning with the landing of paratroops by Fliegerdivision 7 and other units of Fliegerkorps XI in the Maleme–Khania area (the main sector) and at Heraklion and Rethymnon, and proceeding through the transfer of dive-bombers and fighters to Cretan bases, to the sea transport of flak [anti-aircraft] units, supplies, equipment and three mountain regiments of ground troops.[5]

Few commanders in the history of warfare can have had their enemy's plans offered up to them 'on a plate' in such detail and with two weeks' notice. Moreover, any airborne landing, especially by parachute troops, is an extremely hazardous operation, as their descent obviously renders them vulnerable. They depend, above all, on the element of surprise. No wonder the Prime Minister told Wavell that here was a 'heaven sent' opportunity of dealing the enemy a heavy blow.

The 'wizards' of Hut Six continued to find rich gems in the Enigma treasury during the two weeks preceding the invasion (7–20 May) and even during the battle, 'the Enigma contained German situation reports, reinforcement rates, and identification of units landed in the island.'[6] Only the exact size of the invasion force was missing.

As for the preparation to meet the attack, the Official History notes that as well as predicting the probable date of the attack, the Enigma foretold

> that on 19 May the German commanders were to meet with maps and photographs of Maleme, Khania, Rethymnon and Heraklion. These, the areas selected by the Germans for their airborne descents, tallied closely with those to which the British in Crete were already giving prominence in their defence preparations before 7 May, when they learned from the Enigma of the German operational plan. But it was the foreknowledge provided by the Enigma which gave the defenders the confidence and the time to *concentrate all their forces at these points*.[7] [Author's italics]

After all this amazingly good intelligence and astute advance disposition of forces, the reader of the Official History might well begin to assume the invasion repulsed and the battle won. But Crete turned into a disaster for the occupying British and Commonwealth forces, and not without heavy naval losses both during the battle and the subsequent evacuation. The Official History, which is entitled *British Intelligence in the Second World War*, offers no explanation of what went wrong, either militarily or even intelligence-wise, which is odd, as intelligence generally – how it was supplied and understood, its actual content, as well as its subsequent use or misuse – played such a prominent part in the campaign. Instead, we are given a mention of British naval success against two convoys of caiques, without saying that these were carrying just several hundred men, and that the Royal Navy suffered disproportionately heavy losses in both men and ships in destroying or dispersing the second convoy, when they exposed themselves to German air attack.

Among the senior officers arriving on the island from the Greek mainland at the end of April was Major General Bernard Freyberg VC, commander of the New Zealand Division. His 6th Brigade had already left Crete for Alexandria, and he fully expected that other New Zealand units arriving on Crete would soon follow so that he could put his entire expeditionary force together in Egypt. However, Churchill had requested that he was to be in charge of the defence of the island and no one was more astonished than the man himself. According to Antony Beevor, the noted military historian, it was a singularly unfortunate choice.

## Forewarned . . . yet distracted

Churchill had greatly admired Freyberg's bravery and fearlessness in the First World War and was anxious for him to come out of retirement and command the New Zealand Expeditionary Force in 1939. Beevor describes him as a 'first-class trainer of troops' and as having 'a genuine interest in the welfare of his men'. But there were serious weaknesses. 'These failings – chiefly, obstinacy, muddled thinking and an extreme reluctance to criticize subordinates – became especially important in the circumstances of Crete.'[8] 'Freyberg,' comments Beevor, 'provides yet another example of how storybook heroes seldom make good generals.'[9]

Right from the outset General Freyberg appears to have developed what the lawyers call, 'a fixed hopeless settled impression' that the main invasion of the island would be by sea, with the airborne forces playing only a subsidiary role. Soon after being given the command he sent a signal to Wavell in Cairo: 'Forces at my disposal are totally inadequate to meet attack envisaged. Unless fighter aircraft are greatly increased

84

and naval forces made available to deal with seaborne attack I cannot hope to hold out with land forces alone,' and goes on to detail shortages of equipment. A similar signal to the New Zealand Government complains, 'There is no evidence of naval forces capable of guaranteeing us against seaborne invasion.'[10] Beevor points out that expressions such as 'seaborne invasion' suggest enemy landings on the beaches,

> rather than reinforce his airborne troops by sea on a part of the coast he [might have] already captured. They were of course, very different matters. So different were they in the context of the Battle of Crete, that this misunderstanding completely distorted General Freyberg's view of enemy intentions to the point that he misread an Ultra signal on the second day of the battle with disastrous, and almost certainly decisive consequences.[11]

Of course, Wavell, with Admiral Cunningham's backing, assured him that the Navy would support him. But to no avail. It is quite astonishing to think that General Freyberg should not be aware of the broad naval position in the region. That the Royal Navy was in general control of the Mediterranean was common knowledge. There were a few enemy submarines and at points like Crete the Luftwaffe could inflict considerable damage, but it was impossible to envisage a major enemy seaborne invasion that the British Mediterranean Fleet – both surface and submarine – could not and would not thwart. In any case, the enemy simply lacked the necessary troop transports, as was made clear by a signal from Wavell to London on 1 May. This was later confirmed when the enemy was reduced to transporting troops and equipment by caiques. The picture of the 'invincible' Wehrmacht, bristling with modern weaponry, travelling in sailing vessels, was not one likely to appear in Goebbels's inspiring newsreels.

As for Mussolini's boast about 'Mare Nostrum', the naval defeat at the hands of the British at Cape Matapan, just a few months earlier (greatly assisted by very timely deciphering of Italian and Enigma messages at BP,) had made the Italians very reluctant to commit more than token naval forces to assist the Germans.

The Enigma-based information having been so exceptionally good – whether Freyberg was told the true source or whether it was attributed to an agent in Athens – London began to realize from Freyberg's messages that something was amiss. 'The Chiefs of Staff . . . appear to have been disconcerted by Freyberg's back-to-front analysis of the enemy threat . . . this signal was sent to Cairo: "Please enquire from General Freyberg whether he is receiving Orange Leonard [i.e. Enigma-based] information from Cairo if not please arrange to pass relevant OL information maintaining utmost security." '[12]

On 11 May, i.e. after the astonishing Enigma revelations of 6 May, one of the most detailed operational plans ever to be deciphered, 'on Churchill's orders, a senior staff officer, Brigadier Eric Dorman-Smith, was flown [from Cairo] to Crete . . . to brief Freyberg on the accumulated intelligence. Dorman-Smith was impressed by Freyberg's courage but depressed by his tactical sense and 'ruefully put him in his "Bear of Little Brain" category'.[13]

Certainly, as Beevor shows, one or two of the OL signals Freyberg received did appear to shift the emphasis some way towards the seaborne element, although a detailed Air Ministry signal put the matter into perspective by showing the seaborne landings to be a small part of the whole operation. Nevertheless, the General remained completely in the grip of this fundamental misconception and it led to disastrous consequences in his disposition of troops, his tactics and general conduct of the battle, and in particular his failure to defend the Maleme airfield which was crucial to the entire plan. This fixation, already mentioned, resulted in his misreading a vitally important Enigma-based signal which, because of the almost paranoid super-secrecy still surrounding Enigma-based intelligence ('most secret source'), he could not discuss even with his most senior commander.

On 21 May the following signal, OL 15/389, reached Crete:
Personal for General Freyberg          Most Immediate
On continuation of attack Colorado (Crete), reliably reported that among operations planned for Twenty-first May is air landing two mountain battalions and attack Canea. Landing from echelon of small ships depending on situation at sea. . . . In his fixation with a seaborne assault, he seems to have seized upon the words 'Canea' and 'Landing' while forgetting the full stop between them. The idea that an 'echeleon of small ships' intended to land a large force with tanks ... proved a serious mistake.[14]

Freyberg then issued the ill-fated order:

'Reliable information. Early seaborne attack in area Canea likely. New Zealand Division remains responsible coast from west to Kladiso river.

86

Welch Battalion forthwith to stiffen existing defences from Kladiso to Halepa.'

Not only did Freyberg keep the Welch Regiment, his largest and best equipped battalion, in Canea to man the seafront, he would allow no more than the 20th Battalion out of Inglis's 4th Brigade to join the counter-attack on Maleme . . . The counter-attacking force was both too small and too late when in fact Freyberg could have spared five battalions with ample time to crush the enemy at Maleme.[15]

At Bletchley Park the disappointment was intense. Milner-Barry, Head of the Hut Six Watch at the time, writing fifty years later, still felt it keenly.

The Cretan episode was, from the Hut Six point of view, the greatest disappointment of the war. It seemed a near certainty that, with General Freyberg warned that the crucial point of the invasion was to be the airborne attack on the Maleme airport, and the time and every detail of the operation spelt out for us in advance, . . . the attack would be igno-miniously thrown back; and we awaited the operation with anxiety but also with a considerable degree of confidence.[16]

The lesson, all too well illustrated above, is that all intelligence, even the very best, had to be put into the hands of those able and willing to make effective use of it. And this Enigma-based intelligence was the best: authentic, reliable, timely, and in this case practically complete. Ralph Bennett commented that this Enigma-based intelligence 'rarely gave so complete and accurate a forecast again'.[17]

## Tragedy of errors

We have here a tragedy of errors. The super-secrecy surrounding the intelligence which decreed the messages were for General Freyberg's eyes only, meant that he, just one fallible human being, could not discuss them with his closest senior commanders even if he wished to; and they, poor devils, could only conclude that the General's orders, incredible as they may have appeared, must have been based on secret information which he could not, or would not, disclose. In the following August, as we have already mentioned, the new Special Liaison Units came into being and this prevented a repetition of the Cretan disaster. Of course, commanders were not thenceforward obliged to take action on the strength of Ultra intelligence (as it was then called), but at least they had been thoroughly forewarned.

## Notes

1. Calvocoressi, *Top Secret Ultra*, p. 78.
2. Official History, Vol. 1, p. 409.
3. And not its code-name, 'Merkur' (Operation Mercury).
4. Official History, Vol. 1, p. 417. Only a sheer inability to grasp that enemy communications of the utmost secrecy were actually being read, could have led the Chiefs of Staff to consider the reference to Crete as a deliberately misleading message.
5. Official History, Vol. 1, p. 418.
6. Ibid., p. 420.
7. Ibid., p. 418.
8. Beevor, A., *Crete – The Battle and the Resistance*, London, John Murray (Publishers) Ltd., 1991, p. 83.
9. Ibid., p. 84.
10. Ibid., p. 87
11. Ibid.
12. Ibid., p. 88.
13. Ibid., p. 89.
14. Ibid., p. 157.
15. Ibid., pp. 157–8.
16. Sir Stuart Milner-Barry in Hinsley and Stripp, *Codebreakers*, p. 98.
17. Bennett, R., *Ultra and Mediterranean Strategy, 1941–45*, London, Hamish Hamilton, 1989, p. 56.

# Chapter 10

# NORTH AFRICA –
# ULTRA TRIUMPHANT

Bletchley Park's great contribution to the eventual victory in North Africa established the breaking of enemy ciphers as a gift beyond price. Despite Hitler's increasingly heavy involvement in the war against the Soviet Union in 1941–2 he continued to press the British hard in two areas where they were vulnerable – the Middle East and the Atlantic.

General Rommel's Panzer Army too was vulnerable in that it had to be supplied mainly by sea from ports in Italy and Greece. Convoys of supply ships were given air cover by the Luftwaffe and the problem for the British Navy and Air Force was to find them.

Rommel had landed in Africa in February, and during the first half of 1941 BP was reading the Luftwaffe Mediterranean key, which they code-named 'Light Blue'. The convoys of ships with Rommel's supplies were controlled by the Italians with air cover provided by the Germans. The details revealed of these escort flights naturally involved the routes to be taken by the convoys, and this allowed the Navy and the RAF to sink a good deal of Rommel's supplies, and even the tanks for the armoured formations themselves. Even better would have been advance information about convoy routes, the composition of the convoys and the dates of sailing. It may sound a tall order, but some of this too was forthcoming. The Germans had encouraged the Italians to use a version of the commercially-available Swedish Hagelin cipher machine rather than the Enigma. But for whatever reason it was given the advice backfired. Italian book ciphers, which Bletchley had ceased to be able to read, gave way to a machine cipher which, after months of hard work, they were. In June 1941, BP Hut Eight broke this Italian C38M machine system, and a mine of valuable information it turned out to be. Hut Four, who received deciphered naval material from Hut Eight, normally sent their verbatim translations straight to the Admiralty, but now, under pressure of the serious situation, they were allowed to send C38 intelligence direct to Malta and the Middle East.

The C38 traffic was read regularly, without delays, and was on a considerable scale, rising from 600 messages a month in July, 1941, to a maximum of some 4,000 a year later.

The convoys came under attack. In order to protect the source, the convoy would first be 'found' by RAF reconnaissance aircraft, and after its position had been notified, it would be attacked, often by submarines. By the autumn of 1941 enemy shipping was suffering severe losses. Indeed, these sinkings are considered to have halted Rommel's advance and assisted the Eighth Army in forcing him back to El Agheila (Operation Crusader). In the course of this operation Enigma keys were captured from 15 Panzer Army which enabled Bletchley to read the traffic for most of November, before the enemy, realizing what had happened, changed the keys. This 'Chaffinch' key, as BP named it, had several variants, one of which may have been used to advise depots at Rome and Salonika of supplies needed by the Afrika Korps, and one between Army HQ and its corps. This very important key was recovered in the spring of the following year, often needing forty-eight hours to break. Rommel's supply situation at the end of 1941 was 'catastrophic'. 'Between the beginning of July and the end of October [1941] 40 Axis vessels, with a total tonnage of 180,000 tons, were sunk on passage across the Mediterranean, with the result that a fifth of the cargoes loaded in European ports failed to reach North Africa.'[1] The enemy's response was swift. An entire air fleet (Luftflotte 2) arrived; Malta, the principal submarine base, was virtually paralysed ('the most bombed place in the world'), and indeed, in danger of starvation and surrender. Some twenty U-boats were despatched to the Mediterranean – to the intense annoyance of Admiral Doenitz and the great relief of British and neutral shipping in the Atlantic. These measures had their effect and convoys became much more difficult to attack during the winter of 1941/2.

Rommel recovered and went on to achieve another success at Gazala in the following May. Meanwhile, the two sources of valuable shipping information, the Luftwaffe key and the Italian C38, although obviously complementing each other, had not yet been co-ordinated at BP. However, fortune once again favouring BP, a new Naval Section, 3N, was set up in Hut Three early in 1942, probably as a result of the re-organization that set the pattern for the rest of the War. The main purpose of the new watch was to co-operate very closely with the Italian Watch in Hut Four, marrying the Luftwaffe shipping information supplied by Hut Three with the Italian C38 information and then couching the signals in appropriate naval jargon.

## Chaffinch and Phoenix

Shortly afterwards, in April, Hut Six broke the Chaffinch key referred to previously, although with some delay. One of the variants of this key was used for communication between Rommel and Kesselring, the Commander-in-Chief South, in Rome and with Berlin. Another extremely important army key captured at the same time as Chaffinch was 'Phoenix', used between corps and divisions, the main channel through which Rommel controlled his army. Like Chaffinch it was read for a brief period before being changed but in this case was not read again until June 1942. Rommel's successes were only partly due to good generalship and an improved supply position. British field intelligence was distinctly inferior to that of the enemy who deployed a special unit for monitoring British signals, e.g. tank-to-tank. In a similar vein, but even more serious – a positive reverse in the intelligence war – the US Military Attaché in Cairo, Colonel Fellers was having his frequent and precise wireless reports to Washington read by enemy code-breakers so that the Germans were reading Allied intelligence about the Middle East for the first half of 1942.

In May of that year Rommel began his big push from Gazala towards the Nile. The Luftwaffe, although nominally an independent force, was primarily an army-support weapon, a sort of airborne artillery, the very close army-air co-operation proving devastatingly effective in previous campaigns. Hence the presence, previously mentioned, of the air force liaison officers (the 'Flivos') at army HQs. These officers reported to their air HQ the Army's understanding of the military situation, and its future plans, often in detail, so that air operations could be tied in accordingly.

# A friendly scorpion

To coincide with the big push, a new army–air force key, 'Scorpion', came into being for use by the Flivos. It carried a large amount of traffic of great immediacy and at least at the beginning was very easy to break. Indeed, its daily Enigma settings could be worked out in advance – the result of a serious lapse in signal security. What had happened was that another Luftwaffe key, code-named 'Primrose' at BP, which concerned mainly the home districts of the Luftwaffe in Germany, had been broken in January 1942, and when Hut Six tackled the new Scorpion key in April they soon realized, to their utter amazement – and sheer delight – that what they saw before them were old Primrose settings which they had already broken. As it was of the utmost urgency, the Scorpion traffic, quite exceptionally, was intercepted, deciphered and intelligence processed in Cairo, and a small party was sent out from Bletchley. Perhaps the Eighth Army, and its generals, were not all they might have been, certainly not at this point, but the British now had a secret weapon and the authorities were determined to use it.

By June the two German army keys, Chaffinch and Phoenix, were being read with little delay, and with the final addition of one more key dealing with supplies and reinforcements by air, Bletchley became master of all the Enigma ciphers in use in North Africa. The big question, as always, was how would the generals and other commanders make use of this unique intelligence opportunity? Forewarned, as we have already discovered, is not necessarily forearmed.

The first part of 1942 was an exceptionally critical time for the British and their Russian allies. Singapore had fallen in February, and the Japanese were in the process of occupying Burma. The Germans, in May, had begun a powerful advance towards Egypt, and it was not clear whether the Russians could hold the Caucasus. The British were thus faced with the prospect of Rommel's armies threatening Egypt from the west, and victorious German troops from the Russian front entering the Middle East from the north, via Iran. Stalin was pressing Churchill to open a second front in Europe, while Churchill could not even be sure of his oil supplies.

## 'Bomb alley'

To underline this last point the U-boats were returning to the Atlantic and the sinkings, including those of tankers, were mounting month by month,[2] so much so that a crisis was reached by the end of the year 1942. Britain's food supplies were in danger, and the Royal Navy barely had two months' supply of oil! Malta's condition was extremely perilous. If the enemy, after heavy initial losses in Crete, had decided against an invasion by parachute and airborne troops, they could still neutralize the island and its dockyard facilities under the relentless pressure of heavy daily bombing – Sicily's airfields being no more than a few minutes' flying time. Convoys sent to relieve the island had been mainly lost, their naval escorts likewise suffering loss or damage. In August, a convoy of fourteen fairly fast merchant ships, heavily escorted (Operation Pedestal), was counted a success when five ships arrived; one of them, the American Tanker *Ohio*, twice torpedoed, with a crashed aircraft protruding from her deck, and lashed between two destroyers, limped through 'bomb alley' at all of four knots! As well as the merchantmen sunk the Navy lost an aircraft carrier, a cruiser and a destroyer, with a cruiser and an aircraft carrier damaged.

The U-boats which had been despatched from the Atlantic to the Mediterranean the previous autumn had taken their toll, further weakening British naval strength.

## Ultra proves its worth

Then, in the summer of 1942, the British position in North Africa began to improve. Industrial war production was supplying the Army with much-needed modern weapons, and Ultra intelligence of the utmost importance was reaching the commanders following the breaking of the Chaffinch and Phoenix keys. With Rommel already in Egypt following closely behind the Eighth Army, what was called the First Battle of Alamein took place, a limited but decisive engagement in which the German and Italian forces were thoroughly beaten, although not forced to retreat. Auchinleck, the successful commander, was generous enough to admit that without Ultra, Rommel would have got through to Cairo. The army interception service (the Y service) had also assisted in the fighting and was providing valuable tactical information (e.g.

93

identification of unit call signs). Now, it has been argued that Ultra was of limited value in supplying tactical intelligence. If, by 'tactical' is meant hour-by-hour battlefield information, then the Enigma, which was not employed at regimental level, could not serve.[3] But tactics often depend on a knowledge of the enemy's 'state of readiness', and here Ultra was often at its best. In North Africa, the German unit commanders gave their nightly reports, often in the guise of pro-formas, with military abbreviations, to their superiors, stating the numbers of serviceable vehicles, weapons, fuel, ammunition, etc., together with the numbers of equipment destroyed or damaged, those repairable at short notice, and of course, casualties. These pro-formas, once unravelled by Hut Three, could be of the utmost 'tactical' importance to British commanders, who would know, sometimes within hours, of the precise strengths and weaknesses of specific enemy units, assuming they had been identified and located. After another British reverse, it was obvious that Rommel would attack again, before the balance of tank forces changed decisively in favour of the British. In the middle of August he sent a message to Hitler saying he would attack at the end of the month, and giving details of the plan. This was promptly deciphered and delivered within forty-eight hours to General Montgomery, who had just taken command.

The plan showed that Rommel would attempt a manoeuvre that would cut off the Eighth Army from its base, although the Alam Halfa ridge might be a bar to further progress. Montgomery is said to have come to the same conclusion and therefore decided to defend the ridge. Nevertheless, a fortnight's notice of your enemy's intentions together with the date of the attack must be a great boon to any commander, especially one newly-appointed. But this was not all; Ultra intelligence then made possible direct intervention in the struggle. The recovery of the Chaffinch keys filled any gaps in the shipping intelligence, so that a complete picture emerged, with details of sailing dates, loadings of cargoes, routes, air protection and degrees of priority. Selective attacks could then be made against those ships carrying say, tanks, fuel and spare parts, while those transporting food and water, with Allied prisoners in mind, could be spared. Malta, to some extent, was working again; submarines were possibly being restocked and refuelled, the Navy and RAF making a concerted attack on enemy shipping so that nearly half the fuel failed to get through. Indeed, so many tankers were sunk that on 1 September, when the battle commenced, the German and

Italian tanks and other motorized units were frequently held up by lack of fuel making them easy targets for the RAF which was now equal to the Luftwaffe. After two days Rommel withdrew. It was hailed as a victory for the new general, who, however, was not inclined to acknowledge assistance from 'outside sources'. As the doings of Bletchley Park remained largely a closed book for over thirty years after the War, this quite astonishing episode, an outstanding intelligence triumph, did not find its way into the history books.

Rommel could then only wait for the attack to come. At the end of October, at the Battle of El Alamein he was outnumbered by about two to one in tanks, guns and men, and he was further handicapped by fuel shortages, the sinkings in October amounting to nearly half the shipping involved. On 2 November, a few days after defeat, Rommel sent a message to his masters in which he foretold the destruction of his armies:

> After ten days of the hardest fighting against the British who are many times superior on land and in the air . . . the strength of the army is exhausted . . . [and] will therefore no longer be in a position to prevent a further attempt by strong enemy tank formations to break through which may be expected tonight or tomorrow. An ordered withdrawal of the six Italian and two German non-motorised divisions or brigades is not possible in view of the lack of M/T [motor transport] vehicles . . . The slight stocks of fuel do not allow of a movement to the rear over great distances. . . . In this situation . . . the possibility of the gradual annihilation of the army must be faced.[4]

Although on this occasion the British superiority in arms was the winning factor, the above message does bear adequate witness to the effectiveness of the Ultra-led operations which denied the enemy his essential supplies. Moreover, Montgomery was given advance notice of the *effect* the shipping losses would have on Rommel's supply situation, especially in regard to fuel and ammunition. Ultra had again disclosed, in detail, the dispositions of enemy troops beforehand, and the nightly pro-formas, as already outlined, gave a running account of the supply position of many units throughout the battle. Did ever an army have better and fuller information about an enemy – or have its two sister services working so hard on its behalf?

Rommel's army did not suffer the annihilation he had feared. His dire forecast of 2 November may well have anticipated the inevitable outcome that he himself would certainly have imposed had he been the opposing general. If you have your enemy at a severe disadvantage, go in and finish him off; that is how wars are won. But Montgomery was not Rommel; the latter escaped westwards, followed at some distance and at a leisurely pace, by the Eighth Army. Even when Ultra intelligence, on 9 November, informed Montgomery that Rommel had no more than eleven tanks, he declined to attack – although he himself had 280 tanks.

By the middle of February, Rommel found himself between the First Army under Eisenhower, and the Eighth Army's most advanced corps. To avoid being caught between the two he attacked and mauled the American corps (green troops) at the Kasserine Pass, but the First Army was not forced to retreat. At this point bad weather caused Rommel to break off the engagement and he planned to attack Montgomery's forward corps, inflict a serious defeat and send the entire Eighth Army retreating eastwards once more. He intended to attack from the Mareth Line towards Medenine, but his plans were disclosed by Ultra a week beforehand. This time, throwing caution to the wind, Montgomery drove his troops forward by night and day, prepared an ambush with 600 anti-tank guns at the disclosed positions, resulting in the rapid loss of fifty tanks and a notable victory. Rommel realized his plan had been betrayed, but he never knew how!

Early in April the two armies joined up, and a month later came the final surrender of 330,000 men at Cape Bon.

## Notes

1. Bennett, *Ultra and Mediterranean Strategy*, p. 70.
2. To exacerbate an already difficult situation, BP, after six months' successful deciphering, lost the U-boat Enigma after January 1942, so that defensive re-routeing of convoys to avoid the U-boat packs was no longer possible. (See Chapter 11.)
3. From the Gazala battles onward the much-improved Y service may have proved more valuable in actual battle conditions than Ultra.
4. Calvocoressi, *Top Secret Ultra*, pp. 82–3.

# Chapter 11

# THE ATLANTIC – WHERE THE WAR WAS NEARLY LOST!

The Battle of the Atlantic in some ways resembles the Battle of Britain (August/September 1940, when pre-invasion air attacks ceased on the day that British fighter strength was exhausted) – once again with resources stretched to the absolute limit, the whole thing exposing vividly Britain's unpreparedness for war.

As in the Battle of Britain, a point was reached when the enemy withdrew, never again to return in such force. But in this case that point was not reached until May 1943, after nearly four years of gruelling sea war. Meanwhile, British imports of food, of weapons, of raw materials, fell in 1941, and again in 1942, to levels that could have lost the War. Astonishing though it may have seemed to the authorities at the time, Britain, a land renowned for coal and ships, suddenly found itself short of both. The neglect and mismanagement of the coalfields by their owners was proverbial, the shipyards likewise being antiquated and inefficient. Many factors affected British imports. Few foreign ships came willingly to British ports, British ships had to take roundabout routes – especially as the fall of France and the occupation of Norway had brought ships under aerial surveillance and increased the time of voyages by up to 40 per cent. It should be remembered that in 1917 the enormous success the U-boats had was from German bases, and now they had even more strategically placed bases on the French coast. The convoy system actually reduced the speed of ships. When British East coast ports had to close because of enemy action, unloading facilities elsewhere became overstretched or were unsuitable.

It was hardly surprising that imports dwindled. Against a peacetime annual level of imports of some 50 million tons dry cargo (excluding oil), the 1941 figure had slumped to 30 million tons, which was in fact the Government's rock-bottom figure, but the following year was even worse; home consumption exceeded imports by 2.5 million tons, and industry was obliged to draw heavily on its stocks of raw materials. This could have been disastrous, and came about partly because the Admiralty entertained the absurd notion that the development of asdic (submarine detection equipment) had meant the end of the U-boat and partly because Britain entered the War without building up food stocks; wheat, for example, was sufficient for only three weeks. Meanwhile, civilian consumption had been slashed, through food rationing, to levels that could have imperilled the health of the nation by any further cuts. All this shows just how very serious the situation was, and how Germany saw one chance of success after the failure of its air force over Britain and its armies in front of Moscow. Britain might still be bombed and starved, if not into submission, then at least neutralized and knocked out of the War. In this way the Americans could be denied an advance base from which any future invasion of Europe might be mounted. The world is fortunate that a man with the exceptional vision and courage of President Roosevelt was in the White House at that time.

The U-boat started the War, in theory at any rate, in a very strong position. It was extremely difficult to detect and destroy. Better and more strongly-built than those of the First World War, and sailing faster and deeper, they were very hard to see, and apart from a direct hit, were impervious to depth-charges, which had hardly improved in the inter-war years. It might seem surprising, in view of the U-boats' success in the First World War, when they came close to victory, that Germany started the War with so few. Doenitz, the commander of the U-boat fleet, still not ranked higher than Commodore in 1939, and a devoted admirer of Hitler, had argued in the 1930s against the building of big capital ships on the grounds, firstly, that they would not be ready in time, showing how soon they intended to make war, and secondly, that the resources could be far better used to build a fleet of 300 submarines with which to starve Great Britain into surrender. It was a prophetic number because when, as we shall see, the fleet did approach that size, the Allies faced a crisis in the Atlantic. But his argument was not unlike that of the British advocates of strategic bombing – both suggesting that a preponderance of one particular weapon could win a war. Grand Admiral Raeder, the naval Commander-in-Chief, luckily, had greater influence. However, from the Royal Navy's point of view, it was unfortunate that the champions of strategic bombing were able to influence the British Government in the way they did. In the event, Nazi Germany started the War with just 57 U-boats, of which 39 were operational at the outset, but of these only 23 were of the ocean-going type. For the first eighteen months of the War this force actually declined (sinkings over new building), and it was not until the summer of 1941 that new production outpaced losses sufficiently to give the fleet a boost. Even with this depleted force, however, the U-boats did enormous damage, highlighting the awesome fact that Britain was losing ships faster than she could build them. By the end of 1940 losses reached 300,000 tons a month.

This led to the following dilemma: of those ships that were built, how many should carry cargoes and how many should be warships to act as convoy escorts, of which at that time there were precious few – many convoys having as few as two. We have to remember that in 1940 only the naval sloop had sufficient fuel to escort all the way across the Atlantic, and there were not many of those. Anti-submarine escort vessels had to rendezvous with an eastbound convoy at 19° West (about 300 miles off the coast of Ireland). The same applied to escorts from the other side of the ocean, leaving the so-called 'black hole' – which was actually a huge gap – in the middle. Here the U-boats could congregate and operate on the surface with impunity. This partly explains why a small U-boat force could do so much damage. Another reason is that the intelligence contest, at this stage, was entirely in the enemy's favour, BP having had no success against the naval Enigma, whereas the German *B-Dienst* code-breakers were reading a good deal of Admiralty coded wireless traffic and U-boat Command were taking action accordingly.

At the beginning of the War the Admiralty believed, wrongly, that convoys and air patrols would force submarines to operate submerged and in coastal waters. Anti-submarine escorts were thus provided for only a short distance after which a convoy might be escorted for some distance, by other warships.

The U-boat was responsible for two-thirds of all British, Allied and neutral shipping losses during the War – some 14.7 million gross tons, and of this figure half, 7.8 million tons, were lost in the crisis year 1942, some four-fifths of this by U-boat. Of all these sinkings, more than half were in the North Atlantic. On the Allied side, more than 32,000 lives were lost and much serious injury suffered.

The task of safeguarding Great Britain's seaborne supplies fell to the Royal Navy. But the composition of the Navy, its dispositions throughout the world, as well as its old-fashioned leadership, meant that it was not well-placed to carry out its many tasks which would have indicated the following:

1. It had to defend its own bases, none of which was safe, not even Scapa Flow.
2. It had to defend the British Isles which were threatened with invasion until the latter part of 1940.
3. It had to either destroy, or at least try to keep in port and neutralize, the enemy surface fleet.
4. It had to maintain, and when lost try and re-establish, strategic routes in the Mediterranean, including the seemingly impossible task of defending its base at Malta.
5. It was then given the near hopeless mission of escorting convoys to northern Russia ('Every two months?' said the Admiralty; 'Every ten days!' said Churchill.)

To do all this the Navy had an impressive number of capital ships, some sixteen in all, mostly survivors of the First World War, plus a new class of battleship, the *King George V* and her four sister ships, which had been laid down and the first of which was about to be commissioned. It has been said that the decision to build these ships was an obstinate refusal to recognize that the day of the big battleship was over, and the money would have been better spent on aircraft carriers and destroyers. From cruisers downwards the Navy was lamentably short of modern vessels. True, there were sixty-one cruisers, but one-third of these were launched before 1919. Six of the ten aircraft carriers were either conversions or were old, and of these, three were lost soon after the War started. Such a fleet was designed to fight major actions between large heavyweights.

## A sorry tale

Too little attention had been paid to the design of sea-going aircraft, and very few reconnaissance aircraft were available, partly because

RAF Coastal Command was a Cinderella organization, control of which was disputed between the Air Force and the Navy, partly because the machines it might have had were allocated to Bomber Command. These deficiencies were not made good until eventually supplied by the Americans. No one, simply no one, had appreciated that the aeroplane was the natural enemy of the submarine. The magnetic mine, used so successfully in the First World War, had been neglected by the British, but not by the enemy, and at times the Germans were laying mines faster than the British could sweep them. Right through the vital years up to 1943, the Royal Navy was actually short of torpedoes, the most destructive weapon used at sea in the Second World War. Warships did not carry their own direction-finding equipment. Nevertheless the Royal Navy prevailed, despite all these adverse factors and deficiencies, because it was a highly professional, highly motivated, force, and the enemy suffered his own, possibly worse, shortcomings. Lastly, and particularly unfortunate, was the Admiralty's addiction to an old-fashioned, insecure book code, when the other two services had gone over to machine ciphers, which meant that the enemy could and did read British naval signals.

## Intelligence war

If Bletchley Park did well deciphering messages first of the German Air Force and later of the Army, the enemy was doing extremely well against the Royal Navy. As far back as 1935, the *Beobachtungs Dienst*, or *B-Dienst*, the signal intelligence unit of the German Navy, had not only cracked the Royal Navy's most widely-used code, the five-figure Administrative Code, but had broken the more important four-figure Naval Cipher (for officers only) which was super-enciphered to give an additional layer of secrecy. Even in 1935, the *B-Dienst* already employed as many as 500 people, including its headquarters, Tirpitzufer, No. 72, in Berlin, and some twelve or so listening stations, in itself a sinister development, had it been known in the West at the time.

By April 1940, at the time of the German invasion of Norway, it was already reading between one-third and one-half of the messages intercepted in Naval Cipher. After the invasion of Norway, the British C-in-C, Home Fleet, complained, 'It is most galling that the enemy should know just where our ships . . . always are, whereas we generally

101

learn where his major forces are when they sink one or more of our ships.' Hut Eight at Bletchley Park had made no progress at all against the German naval Enigma at this time, and the capture from U-13 of a copy of the naval Enigma procedures later that year must only have depressed them when they realized that the system had none of the weak points BP had successfully exploited in the air force procedure.

By August 1940 enough alarmbells had rung at the Admiralty for them to replace the Administrative Code with a four-figure Naval Code No. 1, and the Naval Cipher with Naval Cipher No. 2, so that for a time *B-Dienst* was less successful. Although the Admiralty had resisted the introduction of machine ciphers, and ships carried code books and subtraction tables, themselves subject to frequent change, they were not necessarily unsafe. But these particular codes did suffer from weaknesses, and there was the further drawback that in the event of compromise by mistakes or capture it is infinitely more complicated to issue new books or tables to ships at sea than it would be to signal the use of a new machine cipher key. In June 1941 Naval Cipher No. 3 came into being, for use between the British, Canadian and US navies, but this too was insecure.

The German Army and Air Force assumed they were the world's greatest, their enemies always retreating, so were not over concerned about cipher security.

The *Kriegsmarine*, on the other hand, knew very well that it was up against a redoubtable foe, the Royal Navy. The enemy knew too that their few capital ships, if they ventured forth, would probably be damaged or sunk, and their submarines would certainly be hunted and destroyed. Thus, like the Poles and the British, theirs was essentially a defensive attitude, so they looked very closely at the security of their signals, especially as they knew that there was a good chance that U-boats or other ships carrying Enigma machines and documents might be captured. The U-boat Command therefore, was extremely cautious. From 1940 to 1943 Doenitz's headquarters lay in three summer villas at Kernaval, a suburb of the port and naval base of Lorient on the southern coast of Brittany from where signals were both sent to, and received from, the U-boat fleet. Unlike the Army and Air Force, only officers were allowed to set the wheels and rings (what the Germans called 'inner settings') of the naval Enigma machines, officers presumably not being susceptible to the blandishments of money or women as would the lower ranks.

Doenitz and his signals staff knew very well that most lapses in signals security were due to human weakness or incompetence, given that the basic procedures were sound, as they certainly were, not to say watertight. The officer having begun the process (wheel order changed every other day), the cipher clerk continued the steps of a more complicated and much more secure procedure than that used by the Army and Air Force. The code books and sheets were split between the officer, who kept the list of settings for the machine, and the cipher clerk, who kept the list of indicators in the wireless cabin. Before messages were sent from the deep bunker at Kernaval they were sent from one end of the room to the other in a dummy run to ensure that any errors would be corrected before transmission. The messages were then retransmitted from a more powerful station near Paris (the old French Colonial Office transmitter) to give the U-boats a second and several subsequent chances of receiving them, because submarines can only receive and transmit signals if on or near the surface. When in hostile waters this might only be at night when they surface in order to charge their batteries. Documents were printed in water-soluble ink on soluble paper.

When a U-boat sighted a convoy it had to make a sighting report. In order to keep this transmission as short as possible, and so frustrate enemy direction-finders and code-breakers, they used the Short Signal Book; this made use of tables which reduced a lot of standard messages to an abbreviated code. After selecting the correct code (e.g. mmpp = intend attack reported enemy force in [grid square]), the operator then re-enciphered his message using the Enigma machine. Despite strong objections from Doenitz, U-boats were obliged to give weather reports, so there was also a Short Weather Cipher (*Wetter kurz Schlüssel*) reducing the commonest types of weather condition to a short cipher which was then further protected by being re-enciphered with the Enigma machine. The Short Weather Cipher was first issued in 1940 as a small booklet consisting of tables each of which condensed an item of a weather report – e.g. air temperature – into a single letter. Even the Enigma procedure itself was shortened. Weather messages could be transmitted in 15-20 seconds and sent at random with no address, just a two-letter signature. Whichever German listening station received them had to forward them instantly to central weather control. The possibility that British meteorological code-breakers might solve their regular weather ciphers caused the Germans to have them re-enciphered using the Enigma.

103

In the event of capture of a German naval vessel it was considered that the British would have to acquire at least four components of the system: the Enigma machine, the list of settings for the machine, the bigram tables and the indicators list. As so many U-boat messages made use of the Short Signal Book, and also the Short Weather Cipher, the acquisition of these would seem almost as essential. It did not seem, even to the super-cautious naval signals authorities, that all components would be captured, although they conceded that the enemy probably had the machine itself. Finally, there was the emergency 'cue word' which would render a captured monthly settings list useless by causing wheel orders and settings to be changed.

Giving a sighting or position report might be thought a breach of the golden rule of as much wireless silence as possible, but Doenitz was committed to his wolf-pack system, and to work effectively it had to be under his control even if it involved extensive use of wireless. Any risk, therefore, would be outweighed by the supreme advantage of central command.

The naval version of the Enigma machine, the Type M (*Schlüssel* M), was more complicated than that used by the Army and Air Force. For example, the three wheels which the officer had to change were chosen from a selection of eight, instead of three out of five in the military version. The significance of this, from the deciphering angle, is that there were now 336 possible wheel orders against just sixty in the military version. There were also three message grades: general (all ranks), officer only (different settings and plugboard connections), and staff (different wheel and ring settings and pluggings). The complicated Enigma operating system worked because just a few hundred carefully trained men were involved. Notwithstanding all this elaborate security, Doenitz and his senior signals staff, Maertens and Stummel, took no chances. They tried to take account of every contingency. When a ship was lost an investigation was held to try to ascertain whether emergency procedures for disposing of Enigma machines and papers had been carried out.

The man who commanded the German U-boat fleet, Admiral Doenitz, a committed Nazi, conducted a campaign of unrestricted submarine warfare, not only against his enemies but particularly against neutrals. At the Nuremberg Trial, after the War, he got ten years for this and for the fact that he did not rescind the order to shoot commandoes and prisoners of war when he became Commander-in-Chief of the entire German Navy in 1943. He was also Hitler's appointed successor. As well as his concept of the wolf-pack, enabling U-boats to operate in mid-ocean, which proved so deadly, he also reversed the conventional practice of attacking in daylight while submerged, and organized surface night-attacks.

From all that has been said so far, it is becoming evident that as many U-boat messages were short and either first coded and then enciphered (Short Signal Book, Short Weather Cipher), or double-enciphered ('officer only' messages), BP was in a quandary. With an increasingly sceptical Admiralty bearing down on them, the urgent problem was how to get hold of those vital documents upon which the Battle of the Atlantic, and therefore the whole course of the War, might depend. The answer was a 'pinch', the capture of an enemy vessel complete with its Enigma code-books and lists intact and legible. A 'pinch' could be accidental or deliberate.

In March 1941, a successful commando raid was carried out against the Lofoten Islands off northern Norway. During the raid an armed enemy trawler, the *Krebs*, was badly damaged in an encounter with the destroyer *Somali* and left burning, stranded on a reef. Some hours later, the *Somali* found it drifting, and the signals officer persuaded the captain, who was not inclined to delay, that there might be something valuable aboard. There was! Like all German naval vessels it carried an Enigma machine and the necessary documents. What they recovered was the Enigma Home Waters key for February 1941. (This was the main key in use at the time, the Foreign Waters key seldom used and never broken.)

The Official History (Vol. 1, p. 337) suggests a 'special effort' was 'concerted' between Naval Intelligence Division and GC&CS, 'in advance of the Lofoten raid' 'to seize the Enigma machine and its settings'. This then, would have been a deliberate 'pinch', but the history fails to mention how they knew of the existence of this small naval vessel, and if they did, why carry out such a devastating initial attack which might easily have sunk her. As it was, thirteen of the crew were killed and the ship left burning and drifting – hardly the action of a commander who had been briefed to recover documents. Compare this with the very deliberate actions against the weather ships when overwhelming force and mock attacks subdued the crews and forced them to abandon ship.

In Kahn, *Seizing the Enigma*, there is a reference to an interview

105

with the Somali's signals officer, Lieutenant Sir Marshall Warmington, which bears out the fortuitous nature of the find, and how he had to persuade his captain to stop and allow them to board the wreck.

## Hut Four recommends a quiet 'pinch'

With the key list recovered from the *Krebs* BP Hut Eight were able, after three weeks of intensive work, to read all the 'back traffic' for February, i.e. a sheaf of intercepted messages which had remained on file in the hope that, one day, they might be deciphered. Now they were able to break the ciphers not only for February, but with some delay, the month of April, then, with delays reduced to about a week, a lot of the May traffic as well. This was BP Naval Section's first breakthrough, these results coming entirely from code-breaking, not from capture, which proved to the deeply sceptical Admiralty that enemy naval Enigma ciphers could indeed be broken. Nothing succeeds like success and Hut Eight were able to recruit much-needed staff. In the back traffic that now became readable, was information about German weather ships. Hut Four's intelligence officers at last had something to get their teeth into. These weather ships, they realized, converted old trawlers though they may be, were carrying the naval Enigma machine and its vital documents. Hut Four recommended a 'pinch' and the Admiralty, having seen good results from the *Krebs*, agreed. To ensure complete success the little ship would have to face overwhelming force and be intimidated into surrender before the documents could be destroyed and before news of the attack could be transmitted. Three cruisers and four destroyers, under Vice-Admiral Holland, all fast, well-armed ships, found the *München* where BP had indicated, and made a mock attack, the shells sending up great plumes of water. The crew abandoned ship, but not before the wireless operator had dropped the Enigma machine overboard. Although the boarding party found no papers in the wireless cabin, Captain Haines, from the Admiralty's Operational Intelligence Centre, knowing of the split between documents kept by the operator and those kept by the officer, went straight to officers' quarters and found what he was looking for. On 10 May 1941 he was able to hand over to Peter Twinn, of BP Naval Section, the list of Enigma settings for June, and even more important, the Short Weather Cipher. The British put out a deliberately misleading message, saying that an

106

armed trawler had been found, and when fire was opened the crew 'abandoned and scuttled their ship' after which they were taken prisoner.

This message was duly noted by the enemy, but no enquiry was ever held, nor any changes made in cipher procedure. At that time German Naval Command, North, busily preparing to attack the Soviet Union, somehow ignored the fate of a small ship. A serious error. The capture of the special Short Weather Cipher, as used by the U-boats, was of singular importance at that moment. Just a little earlier, BP's Meteorological Section, led by Professor McVittie, in Hut Ten, had broken the Kriegsmarine's regular weather cipher. This was based on representations of weather factors such as pressure and temperature, using the symbols of the existing international weather code, but carefully disguising them in a cipher and listing them in tables. These sets of five tables were reissued as often as five times a day, with changes each time. This cipher is not the same as the Short Weather Cipher used by U-boat Command (mentioned previously), the abbreviations of which were designed to reduce transmission times to short bursts lasting about fifteen seconds, thus giving an enemy little chance of a direction-finding 'fix'. All German weather information, e.g. from submarines or aircraft, had to be forwarded immediately to central weather control. This body would often retransmit the information, using the regular weather cipher, to all units.

Having thus broken the regular weather cipher and also having captured the Short Weather Cipher, Hut Ten could compare the plain-text version of the regular weather broadcast with what must be the same information sent by the U-boats. This was a wonderful aid to deciphering those frustratingly short U-boat messages. These recipherments (same or similar information in two cipher systems) were to become BP's principal means of attack on the U-boat Enigma. Another very useful source of recipherments was the Dockyards and Fairways cipher (WS), a hand cipher used by small auxiliary vessels as well as in dockyards. As mentioned earlier, this too was broken regularly from the spring of 1941. If a message was put out (to give urgent warnings of storms or enemy mines), having broken one system, say WS, BP would have a first-rate crib ready to attack the Enigma. Such opportunities were referred to as 'kisses'. The work on Dockyard, difficult and tedious – and those beavering away at it felt as if they were in a 'Cinderella' organization – was, nonetheless, a vindication of

Bletchley's policy of attacking everything, regarding nothing as unimportant, and always looking for connections between the different parts of the enemy's signal intelligence, which, after all, reflected the structure of his war machine.

## The RAF tries a little gardening

Examples of recipherments, duly broken, were put on display when BP needed to advertise its wares, e.g. to impress distinguished, but still slightly sceptical, visitors. So important were recipherments to a section usually starved of cribs that the RAF were occasionally asked to sow mines deliberately, simply in the hope of generating warnings in both Dockyard and Enigma. The request was for 'gardening'. (BP probably knew the minesweepers carried only Dockyard.)

The *Kriegsmarine* used more than 20 hand ciphers, 6 of them carrying high grade (i.e. high security) information, of which 3 were read, usually without delay. Dockyard was the most well known, but there was also the *Reservehandverfahren* (RHV), used as a stand-by in case of Enigma failure. They were invaluable as a source of cribs and sometimes of intelligence.

## A prize emerges from the waves

Just two days after the *München* was captured, the U-boat, U-110, was forced to the surface on the other side of Iceland by warships of Escort Group 3 under Commander Baker-Cresswell. The U-110 was one of the latest Atlantic U-boats, Type IXB, 1,050 tons, cruising distance 12,400 nautical miles, top speed 18.4 knots on the surface, 7.3. knots submerged. It could dive to 330 feet, having submerged in just over half a minute, and was armed with twenty-two torpedoes. Under the command of a certain Lieutenant Lemp, who had acquired the dubious distinction of having sunk an unarmed passenger liner, the *Athenia*, on the very first day of the war, the U-110 had just sunk two merchant ships, the *Bengore* and the *Esmond*, when it was surprised by Baker-Cresswell's destroyer *Bulldog*, and the corvette *Aubretia*, whose pattern of depth-charges badly damaged the boat. Suddenly, the U-boat began to move towards the surface, either because the captain had succeeded in blowing the tanks, or, more probably, it had been pushed upwards by the explosions beneath it. The crew of the U-110, expecting at one moment to be descending to a watery grave, and the next instant finding themselves on the surface being fired at by three warships at close range, abandoned ship.

Now, the story goes that at the sight of the loathsome vessel Baker-Cresswell gave orders to fire prior to ramming, a common way of finishing off a U-boat on the surface. However, when he saw the crew attempting to abandon ship he suddenly changed his mind and ordered all three ships to cease fire. The third ship, the destroyer *Broadway* was making straight for the submarine with the obvious intention of ramming, and it was this that may have prompted the order to abandon ship. What may have made Baker-Cresswell change his mind was the recollection that when at Naval College in the 1920s, he had been told of the code-book captured from the German light cruiser *Magdeburg* in 1914, and what a very valuable find this had been. A complete submarine within his grasp, a naval 'prize', he decided to have the boat boarded. The speed of events had been such that everything had been left in perfect order, and the emergency procedures for disposing of Enigma material had not been carried out. Much equipment, and on Baker-Cresswell's orders, documents, were removed. When the *Bulldog* reached Scapa Flow, Bletchley sent up two men with a briefcase; in fact, there were two packing cases to be examined. The most important items were photographed and the pictures left at the base, just in case their plane should crash on its way south. The Bletchley men were taking no chances, for the booty included the vital Short Signal Book, used in sighting, position, fuel, and other reports – in fact the bulk of the traffic – together with the special settings used in 'officer only' messages, not to mention the 'cue-word' system, a fail-safe arrangement which would have changed all settings in case of an emergency such as this, but, unluckily for the enemy, had remained inoperative. These were all invaluable items which the planned captures had failed to yield.

## Who sank the *Bismarck*?

Despite all precautions, suspicions were sometimes raised in the minds of Doenitz and his staff about the security of their signals. When the re-routeing of convoys began in the spring of 1941, they began to wonder, but the most alarming cause of suspicion arose after the sinking of the *Bismarck* in May. Together with the heavy cruiser *Prinz Eugen*, the *Bismarck* was about to embark on a 'cruise' that would have resulted in enormous damage to British and neutral shipping. The *Bismarck*, a new, fast battleship, embodying the latest technology, and the most powerful ship on either side, was giving the Admiralty a nightmare. They had good reason to be alarmed. Less than a week after leaving port the two ships sank the cruiser *Hood* and damaged the very modern *Prince of Wales*. But the *Bismarck* itself was twice damaged later that day (24 May 1941) and leaking fuel, it decided to make for Brest. The British forces lost track of the *Bismarck* and it might well have reached port unimpeded had the ship not signed its own death warrant. Breaking the golden rule of wireless silence on such an occasion, it transmitted a half-hour-long message which very foolishly betrayed its position, all Admiralty direction-finding resources concentrating on it. At BP deciphering of naval signals had only recently begun, was still sporadic and subject to delay, and the long message was not read. But later, the signal was repeated, being sent from Berlin to Athens in a Luftwaffe key which was deciphered by Hut Six on the evening of the 25th, showing the *Bismarck* heading for France. By then however, the ship's position and course were known and were finally determined by a Catalina aircraft, although the BP information had given additional confirmation.

There are stories still to be found in print, to the effect that BP, or even Harry Hinsley, 'sank the *Bismarck*'. Now the Official History, of which Sir Harry was himself the chief editor, makes no such claims. It does mention that deciphering the naval Enigma made only one contribution, and that concerned helping to raise the alarm, on 21 May, about the presence and danger of the two enemy warships, which were also sighted at about the same time.

BP Naval Section, in the person of Harry Hinsley, did find one important piece of evidence on 24 May, the day of the naval engagement. His monitoring of the German naval wireless system (traffic analysis) showed that the wireless control station for the *Bismarck* had been switched from Wilhelmshaven to Paris, a strong indication that the battleship was making for the safety of a French port, at a time when the Admiralty was uncertain of the *Bismarck*'s intentions, unaware that she had sustained damage, and so were unable to dispose forces to meet her. However, there is no record of the time this message was passed to the Admiralty's OIC, or whether the information was acted upon. According to German records the switch of stations was about midday. Even if, as the more fanciful stories suggest, Hinsley's warning was ignored (a certain distaste for Bletchley, it is said, still being prevalent in the OIC), by 10.23 the following morning (25 May) as the Official History points out, the Admiralty had ordered Force H to move up from Gibraltar on the assumption that the enemy battleship was heading for Brest, and this proved correct. Moreover, the *Bismarck*, not realizing that it had shaken off the British ships shadowing it – and assuming that they must still be aware of its position – incautiously sent three more signals on the morning of the 25th, and it was the direction-finding bearings and other characteristics of these signals that finally led to the right decision about the *Bismarck*'s course. The History also points out that by around 18.00 on the 25th all the British fleet concerned were pursuing the *Bismarck*, and the deciphering of the long message by Hut Six shortly afterwards was no more than confirmation of what was already known. In any case, the History adds, aerial reconnaissance would probably have found her, and in fact at 10.30 on the morning of 26 May, the *Bismarck* was sighted by the Catalina, and at 11.15 by a carrier aircraft from Force H.

It was then a matter of whether the battleship could be slowed down and engaged before it reached the approaches to Brest and air cover. On the evening of the 26th aircraft from *Ark Royal* struck twice with torpedoes, one of which very luckily jammed the rudder, and the *Bismarck* was sunk the following morning.[1]

As to Hinsley's 'How I sank the *Bismarck*' as his Cambridge college talks were sardonically referred to (see p. 70), if his evidence had been acted upon immediately – and not simply been put in the intelligence pot with other items of information – about twenty hours might have been saved. But this did not happen and a better title for the talks would have been, 'How I might have sunk the *Bismarck*'.

To suggest, as some still do, that news of BP's part in the sinking, 'swiftly got around' and 'raised morale' at the Park, is to fail to understand how Bletchley worked. No one spread anything around; they were all too acutely aware of the high security risk, even had there been no strict rules. I recently mentioned this to a BP veteran who had worked in the Manor House and all he knew about the *Bismarck* was what he had heard on the BBC news. Of course, several sections at Bletchley were involved, but they would not have been aware of the comparatively small part BP had played in the total operation, as the overall picture was known only to the Admiralty. But a hare was started, and seemingly still runs.

## Too much excitement for the Admiralty

Prior to *Bismarck*'s leaving port, five fuel tankers, two supply ships and two small scout ships had been stationed at widely-scattered points to ensure she could stay at sea for a long time. Bletchley, who had had just begun to decipher naval Enigma, were able to give the Admiralty the precise locations of all of them. Perhaps in a heady flush of excitement at this new miracle of intelligence, the Admiralty decided that all but two should be found and sunk, the two allowed to remain presumably to avoid raising suspicion! Within three weeks all the ships had been sunk or captured. Fate had delivered the over-zealous Admiralty a sharp shock, for British warships, quite by chance, had discovered and disposed of the remaining two. This was a flagrant breach of the security rule that Enigma-based intelligence was only to be used if 'thoroughly camouflaged' and the source not prejudiced. That ships so far apart, in such remote places and in such a short time (five of them in three days), could have been found, looked very suspiciously like deciphering German signals.

After giving a lecture on this topic the author was approached by a former naval chief petty officer who remembered that they had found a German tanker in a remote part of the Atlantic soon after the sinking of the *Bismarck*. 'I remember we had more prisoners on board than crew,' he said, and then, 'was that Bletchley Park telling the navy where to find it?' 'Of course it was,' the author replied. 'I've always wondered about that,' he said.

## . . . and too much for the *Kriegsmarine*

This was all too much for the German naval authorities, who immediately launched a lengthy investigation. All the precautions were exhaustively considered but were finally exonerated, deciphering by theoretical means alone, sheer analysis, was declared impossible. This was a 'close run thing' if ever there was, and BP Naval Section must have been expecting major changes in enemy cipher procedure at any moment, and they had only just got going, nearly two years into the war! Official clearance notwithstanding, two moderate changes to improve security were made to the cipher procedure. One was to further disguise the position of U-boats at sea. This had been done by grid references, with the map of the ocean divided into squares with two letters and four figures indicating the square and position (in latitude and longitude). This was now altered with letters transposed, using the bigram substitution tables already used by U-boats to encipher Enigma indicators (see Appendix 3). This substitution system, known only to U-boat Command, excluded the rest of the *Kriegsmarine* from September 1941. It was a clumsy, half-hearted move, and so complicated that it sometimes confused U-boat commanders.

An entirely new system of disguising geographical position was to follow in December, one that was to prove a big headache for BP. In August, Doenitz had begun to address his U-boats no longer by the number of the boat but by the name of the commander. BP responded by keeping lists of these men, and, where possible, a file on each. Then, in October 1941, the U-boats were further separated from other branches of the Navy by no longer using the Home Waters key, but having an exclusive new key of their own. This was called Triton[2] by the Germans, and, appropriately enough, Shark, by BP. This altered the settings from the regular key, and was introduced partly to deter internal spies – and perhaps external eavesdroppers – and partly because too much traffic in one key is always risky.

Action was also taken on the British side. From mid-1941, soon after these naval actions, all wireless signals sent by the Admiralty which were based on Ultra intelligence, were sent by 'one-time pad' (to be used once only), an unbreakable if cumbersome, system.

By the spring and summer of 1941 things were looking up for Hut Eight and the Naval Section. After the long barren months with no results and an increasingly sceptical Admiralty – even dark hints that they might be displaced or taken over – the early part of 1941 saw a wonderful flowering of much previous hard work coupled with some very lucky breaks. The Bletchley formula of 'attack everything, overlook nothing, use the best brains intensively, round-the-clock if necessary – and hope for a stroke of luck' was now working for Hut Eight as it had for Hut Six a year earlier. A summary of some of the events so far described may now be useful.

In February, the Meteorological Section (Hut Ten) headed by Professor McVittie, broke the German Navy's regular Meteorological Cipher after many months of hard work. Early in March came the Lofoten Raid and the lucky capture of Enigma papers from the *Krebs*. No sooner had this given Hut Eight its first break into the Enigma traffic, revealing the presence of the weather ships, when the hand cipher section of Hut Four, after a long hard slog, cracked the Dockyard Enigma (WS).

The capture of the Short Weather Cipher, as used by the U-boats, from the weather ship, the *München* in May, complemented perfectly the breaking of the regular weather cipher by Hut Ten. It was realized that the short weather signals from the U-boats were often rebroadcast by the Germans in the regular weather cipher that had been broken by Hut Ten. In this way, Hut Ten's decipherments produced the meteorological plain text and this was the same information that had been put out by the U-boats. This provided good cribs for the Bombes. But that was not the end of the matter. The greater difficulty lay in tracking down the particular U-boat message that had originated the rebroadcast, but Huts Ten and Eight managed even this, making the 'kiss' complete. Hut Ten's liaison man with Hut Eight in these matters was Philip Archer – so these achievements were called 'Archery'.

'Kisses' resulting from re-encipherments, or recipherments, also arose when the same message was issued in both Dockyard and Enigma, the originators seeming neither to know nor care about the dangers of such procedure (although it broke a basic cipher rule), and could have been prevented, or made less risky, by rephrasing the texts of the messages. The capture of the Short Signal Book and special 'officer only' settings from the U-110, almost completed the 'armoury' of code-breaking weapons available when, without benefit of further capture, Hut Eight would have to face the enemy alone.

As a result of all the captures, and of the deciphering thus made possible, Naval Section was now able, for the first time, to send the Admiralty vital operational information, although, at the outset, with unacceptable delays between intercepting messages and teleprinting the final result, of anything from thirty-four hours (just possible) to eleven days. In June, however, after the more recent captures, times of solution and despatch were down to under six hours. But when the captured keys ran out, they would again face long delays.

A further capture was called for. On 28 June 1941, another weather ship was captured. Half-hidden among the icebergs of the Norwegian Sea, around the 72nd parallel, the cruiser *Nigeria*, and three fast destroyers, 'found' the *Lauenberg* and 'bombarded' it with practice shells. With the noise and smoke (specially added) and awesome warships bearing down at speed, the crew took to the lifeboats. The capture was timed deliberately for the end of June, in order to obtain the cipher sheets for the month of July, and the plan worked.

A further reason for this final deliberate capture, although not acknowledged, was possibly to obtain a further set of bigram tables, without which the tantalizing game of Banburismus could not continue to engage the high-powered mathematical intellects of Hut Eight. From September 1941, those same bigram substitution tables – as mentioned previously – would also be used to disguise further the German naval grid code which indicated (or revealed) the position of a U-boat.

By early August, Hut Eight was entirely on their own, and to begin with, were slow. The very short messages, often double-enciphered, the tight procedures and absence of mistakes, all made life difficult. If there were no recipherments, the short messages, yielding poor cribs or none, required maximum use of Banburismus and of Bombes, which might have to be run for days on end. The two sections of Hut Eight, although collaborating very fully, were stretched to the limit. The Bombes were in very short supply. Indeed, by the end of June 1941, the number was as small as six, 'of which at least one was always available for naval work'. One! In this scandalous situation deals would have to be struck between the Heads of Huts Six and Eight as to which signals were the more urgent. Hut Eight was short of staff, even to operate the few Bombes available, i.e. on a twenty-four hour basis, and was generally suffering from management failure, as BP had grown too big and complex for the small cosy pre-war establishment.

In the spring of 1941 the U-boats intensified their attacks on the shipping lanes of the North Atlantic, and the British authorities became very anxious in case imports fell to dangerous levels. The U-boat Command adopted wolf-pack tactics, attacking on the surface at night, tactics which – like so much else – took the Admiralty by surprise, although as the Official History points out, they were publicly advocated by Doenitz in a book before the war. On the other hand, two other sources of heavy loss to merchant shipping, surface raiders and the Luftwaffe, now diminished, the surface raids having been suspended and the aircraft gradually withdrawn for operations in southern Europe, North Africa and the Soviet Union. This enabled the RAF to take a better grip on the Western Approaches.

Despite this improvement the Official History suggests that the U-boat offensive would have reached 'crippling proportions' if losses in the second half of the year had continued to expand at the rate of those in the first half. Thankfully, the latter part of the year saw a substantial drop. 'In the four months to the end of June they had sunk shipping at the rate of 282,000 tons a month . . . from July to the end of the year their monthly total averaged 120,000 tons.'[3]

From 18 June the Admiralty increased the minimum speed for independently routed ships (not in convoy) to fifteen knots, and there followed a 'dramatic decline' in the loss of such ships – e.g. from 120 in April-June down to twenty-five between July and September, and this, says the history, is the main cause for the 'reduction in actual shipping losses'. The History had already mentioned that 'great improvements both in organisation and equipment were now being made to the British defences.'[4]

Nevertheless, 'The difference between what the U-boats achieved over-all and what they might have achieved – and indeed, expected to achieve – was due to the great improvement in the evasive routeing of the convoys that took place when GC&CS began to read the naval Enigma.'[5] Although there were interruptions in the reading of the Enigma owing to 'operational circumstances' and 'technical difficulties', 'There was to be a close correlation between the periods when [the interruptions] were being encountered and those in which the performance of the U-boats temporarily recovered.'[6]

Despite deciphering difficulties, reading the Enigma had so improved re-routeing that 'U-boats in the North Atlantic made no sightings between the beginning of the month (June) and 23 June.'[7] and 'In July the U-boats on the trans-Atlantic routes again patrolled for three weeks without seeing a convoy.'[8] In August, although deciphering was up to three days in arrears, the U-boats again found nothing for ten days from 10 August.

In September, however, the U-boats achieved a considerable degree of success, sinking thirty-four ships, partly, the history tells us, as a result of an increase in their numbers, but mainly because a new method of disguising the U-boats' positions at sea in the Enigma messages (already described) which was introduced on 11 September, created difficulties and delays.

In October, the U-boats attacked only one trans-Atlantic convoy (SC48) and one convoy on the north-south route . . . Allied shipping losses were cut back by twenty-five percent from the September level. And in November this comparative decline in the rate of the U-boat successes was followed by a landslide. The U-boats sank in that month only 62,000 tons of shipping . . . For this debacle, which marked the defeat of the U-boat Command in the major offensive against the convoys . . . the growing expertise of the OIC in evasive routeing, based on the reading of the Enigma, was a fundamental cause.[9]

## U-boat offensive falters

There is however, more than one view about the value of reading the naval Enigma at this stage of the Battle of the Atlantic. 'The captured documents from the U-110 and the two weatherships and the subsequent acceleration of [deciphering] solutions had no immediate direct effect on the Battle of the Atlantic. In June 1941, when solution times declined to three or four hours, roughly the same number of tons succumbed to U-boats as in May, when solution times ran to three or four days.'[10] The same applied to July, which was fast, and August, which was slow. 'In fact, in the fast-solution months of June and July, U-boats sank almost exactly the same tonnage in the North Atlantic as in the slow-solution months of May and August . . . intelligence did not always rule in the war against the U-boats. Other factors outweighed it. The July–August loss of tonnage fell to under a third of the May-June figure for reasons unrelated to BP.'[11]

Some of the 'other factors' had been mentioned by the Official History, some not. They include: convoys now being escorted right across the Atlantic; escorts had become more experienced and efficient; the minimum speed for 'independents' had been raised; more air cover had become available; Hitler, at that point, was anxious not to provoke the United States by attacking American-escorted convoys; the new U-boat captains lacked experience; U-boats were being withdrawn to other theatres of war; escort ships were gradually being fitted with radar for short-range U-boat detection, as well as high-frequency direction-finding equipment.

In order to consider the 'defeat of the U-boat Command' it would be reasonable to ask whether any substantial destruction of U-boats had taken place, and the size of the fleet heavily reduced, as happened in 1943. It had not. By 'defeat', however, the history probably implies, not defeat in battle, but more a 'blunted offensive', a strategic planning failure. For this notable lack of success by the U-boats from July to November 1941, the history claims that 'evasive routeing based on the

117

reading of the Enigma was a fundamental cause.' It was certainly a contributory factor, but there were others. U-boats, whose numbers were not yet large, were being withdrawn from the Atlantic throughout the summer and autumn of 1941. Apart from those sent to the Baltic for the war against the Soviet Union, which began in June, the very success of the Navy and RAF, guided by Bletchley Park, in sinking Rommel's supply ships in the Mediterranean, caused U-boats to be despatched to that theatre, a total of twenty having been sent by mid-December. By October or November, a number of boats would have been withdrawn for refitting in preparation for a long voyage to the American East coast, pending the concentrated attack on shipping that would follow Hitler's declaration of war against the US early in December. This would entail the most experienced captains and crews.

The Official History acknowledges the disappearing U-boat, but sticks to its guns.

> If the main reason for the lack of sightings by U-boats during November was that the flow of Enigma intelligence into the OIC about their dispositions was so complete, another reason was that, . . . the number [of U-boats] on patrol in the Atlantic and the number on passage to and from their patrol areas, was declining on account of the withdrawal of U-boats from the Battle of the Atlantic to the Mediterranean and to Norwegian waters.[12]

> In September twenty U-boats had been on patrol in the Atlantic . . . On 1 November there were ten in the north Atlantic and six off Gibraltar.[13]

> On 22 November . . . it [U-boat Command] ordered all U-boats to concentrate in the Gibraltar area and virtually abandoned the offensive against the trans-Atlantic convoys.[14]

> and on 20 December, when there were five [U-boats] in the north Atlantic but when four of them were known to be on passage to the Mediterranean, the OIC's U-boat situation report commented that, 'the primary object seems, at least temporarily, to be no longer the destruction of merchant shipping'.[15]

This seems a strange comment, for the history, without explanation or seeming discomfort, immediately goes on to record that, 'Despite the decline in the number of U-boats on patrol, the shipping sunk by U-boat in the Atlantic increased in December 1941; twenty merchant ships were lost there'[16] (and in the attack on convoy HG 76 the aircraft carrier HMS *Audacity* was sunk). This same 'defeated' U-boat Command went on to account for some 327,000 tons of shipping in January 1942.

Clearly the fortunes of war had spoiled the second half of the U-boat Command's 1941 offensive, as its submarines were needed elsewhere, but by December it was beginning to recover. Perhaps 'tactical retreat' might be more accurate than 'defeat'. Some of the 'brass' in Whitehall, noting the low shipping losses in November, concluded that the 'U-boat problem' had been 'solved', little realizing the factors involved, or that the following year, 1942, was to be the black year, in which losses quadrupled in the second half (from 600,000 tons in the latter half of 1941 to 2,600,000 tons in the second half of 1942), again threatening Britain's lifeline.

## A touch of the midnight sun

Hitler was known to have a phobia about an Allied 'threat' to Norway. If the German forces could not cross the Channel in order to invade Britain in 1940, how he imagined the British could brave the North Sea and the hazardous journey to Norway, is difficult to understand. But then the mind of the mass-murderer was very hard to fathom. The probability is that he was aware of the implacable hatred of almost the entire Norwegian population, and was afraid they would rise as one given the opportunity. In October 1941, a Northern Waters group of U-boats was formed on his personal orders, and he insisted that eight U-boats be kept stationed in the Iceland–Scotland area to defend the Norwegian coast. During March the number of this group had risen to twenty-four, probably causing extreme irritation to Doenitz, and certainly preventing their deployment off the American coast.

This obsession never left Hitler, and about twelve divisions of no doubt extremely thankful troops were kicking their heels there until almost the end of the War. The British played up to this madness, and in 1944, before D-Day, created a phantom army, the so-called 'Fourth Army' in Scotland, in order to foster the illusion. But the deception did not succeed in getting further German reinforcements sent to Norway.

It might be thought that the outstanding successes in reading the enemy's air and now naval signals traffic had put Bletchley Park, by late 1941, in a commanding position in the field of intelligence. But Britain's

119

military and economic situation remained perilous. If the Nazi advance into the USSR, then proceeding rapidly, should result in a Soviet collapse or surrender, Britain could expect a renewed enemy attack with vast forces released from the Eastern Front. Despite these dangers, much of the pre-war attitude to intelligence remained, the War Office in particular continuing to resent BP's control over the results of decoding, and alone among the three services continuing to conduct its own traffic analysis, although an official enquiry had confirmed the obvious fact that code-breaking and traffic analysis were inseparable. BP still had only eight Bombes which needed to be run twenty-four hours a day, but there were not sufficient operators for three shifts, and there was a shortage of other staff which was actually slowing down the work. The pre-war Director of GC&CS, Alistair Denniston, kindly, but other–worldly and indecisive, was still in charge, the organization of BP generally failing to reflect the all-out war raging outside. To leading people at BP, knowing what they did of the enormous value of their contribution to the war effort, the situation was intolerable, and called for drastic measures.

In September 1941, Churchill had paid a visit to BP and had met some of the senior boffins whom he is said to have praised as 'the geese that laid the golden eggs and never cackled'. Churchill was already enjoying the benefit of these eggs. At his special request a selection of decoded messages was sent to him every day in a buff-coloured box to which the Prime Minister kept the key. As intelligence co-ordinating and presenting was still in some disarray among the Whitehall departments, this special insight meant that the PM was probably the only person with a special knowledge of certain defence matters and this put him in a strong position regarding his own advisers, who however, were worried that he may not have understood the background or the implications of the many signals he received from BP, and that he might take ill-considered action on the strength of them, which he almost certainly did. Naturally, Churchill had a special regard for those who maintained this miraculous daily supply. What he did not know was that his geese were about to complain, if not to cackle.

## Action this day

In the middle of October, having met the PM, and hoping that some of their names might have stuck, four of the leading code-breakers, two each from Huts Eight and Six, decided to make a direct approach to the man at the top. The letter, drafted by Gordon Welchman, set out, in plain language, some of the difficulties facing them. They pointed out that work was being held up, or not being done at all, because of staff shortages, and the reason for their direct approach was that 'for months we have done everything that we possibly can through the normal channels, and that we despair of any early improvement without your intervention.' They go on to list particular problems and complaints, e.g. where shortage of staff was delaying the solution of naval ciphers and of Luftwaffe ciphers in North Africa, as well as inability to operate or 'test' the 'Stories produced by the bombes' except by using staff needed elsewhere, as the promised Wrens (WRNS – Women's Royal Naval Service) had not appeared. They also hinted darkly about 'unnecessary impediments' in other directions, suggesting the internal organization and administration, although Commander Travis, the Deputy, was pointedly exonerated from any such criticism. The letter, headed 'Secret and Confidential Prime Minister only' was dated 21 October 1941, and signed by Turing, Welchman, Alexander and Milner-Barry – the heads of Huts Eight and Six, and their respective deputies, the last-named being charged with delivering it in person.[17]

The letter had an immediate effect. Churchill sent a memorandum to General Ismay headed 'ACTION THIS DAY.' Within a month the head of the Secret Service reported to Churchill that everything was being done, and although Welchman was ticked off for taking the direct route, an investigation into BP's internal affairs was, nonetheless, initiated (see also Appendix 4). One immediate result was that in the following February an internal reorganization replaced Denniston with Travis. Whitehall was astonished to discover that the 'woolly jumper brigade' were not the clever, if unworldly, back-room boys they had imagined, but also possessed political skill and were a force to be reckoned with.

## Darkness at Bletchley

The German naval M4 Enigma cipher machine came into service on 1 February 1942, having taken over a year to design, produce and install in all ocean-going U-boats. It was not the quick response to U-boat Command's suspicions in the latter part of 1941 that is sometimes suggested. U-boats operating in coastal waters, for security reasons, were not supplied with the new machine. In fact, it was not really a new machine, but a clever modification of the existing naval Enigma, a classic wartime 'Mark II'. A fourth wheel had been added but it did not revolve with the other three. Previously, the naval Enigma machine settings had offered a choice of three wheels to be selected out of eight, giving 336 possible wheel orders. Had the new wheel been made an integral part of the machine, revolving with the others, there would have been a choice of four out of nine, giving 3,024 possibilities, and the settings of the new wheel would have added a further twenty-six times increase as well, probably resulting in an impregnable system.[18] Even so, the problem had become twenty-six times as bad as before (although not 234 times as bad). In fact, Bletchley had already discovered the wiring of the new fourth wheel. As was often the case, this came about by being quick to spot and then exploit, an enemy blunder. During the latter part of 1941, as the M4 machines were gradually being installed, the new wheel was kept in a neutral position. On one fatal occasion a cipher clerk had accidentally moved it out of position and the resulting 'gobbledygook' was noted at BP – as was the necessary retransmission in the normal setting which BP was currently reading. This was sufficient for Hut Eight to be able to work out the wiring of the new wheel. Thus armed, Hut Eight was able to break the traffic for two or three days in February and March 1942, because the same messages had also been put out in another key which was being read. But, and a very big but, because of the difficulties mentioned in deciphering messages using the four-wheel Enigma, and despite the good cribs available, it took six (three-wheel) Bombes seventeen days to find the settings. This would hardly suit the Tracking Room with their urgent need for U-boat information within twenty-four to thirty-six hours of interception.

One of the messages so gratuitously and rashly enciphered in more than one key was the news, clearly intended to boost the morale of all personnel, that Doenitz had become an admiral!

Despite the limited nature of the changes introduced, this was the most significant development in German code-making during the Second World War. Although designed to defeat internal spying and treachery, it had a powerful side-effect that could never have been imagined. The arrival of M4 simply devastated Hut Eight which had been only just keeping up with enemy changes, and the last change, the 'address book' system of disguising the actual positions of U-boats at sea, had still not been solved when the blow fell on 1 February. Their work was shattered and not all the genius of Alan Turing, Hugh Alexander, Jack Good, Peter Twinn, Peter Hilton and the rest could put it together again. Bletchley would have needed twenty-six Bombes to do the work of one, or have some four-wheel Bombes which simply could not be developed quickly or at all easily.

Naval Section was not completely in the dark; intelligence was still forthcoming, in goodly measure, from those parts of the Kriegsmarine still using the Home Waters key, the Mediterranean key or hand ciphers such as Dockyard. But it had little bearing on the U-boat war, where, with the Shark key enciphered on the four-wheel machine still unbroken, the advantage lay entirely with the enemy. M4 could not have come at a worse time – a time of deepening crisis when monthly shipping losses of half a million tons or more, were reached.

## Notes

1. A teleprint from Hut Four to the Admiralty (ZTP/902) reported the fatal signal – that the ship had suffered *'torpedotreffer achteraus'* – torpedo strike astern, but this was only deciphered after the *Bismarck* was sunk.
2. Although the Official History mentions key changes in October 1941, it maintains that the Shark key (Triton) was introduced in February 1942, to coincide with the arrival of the new four-wheel Enigma. This is disputed by Kahn in *Seizing the Enigma*, p. 306, where he quotes official records, both British and German, to show that 'Triton carried U-boat messages enciphered in three-rotor Enigma . . . well before 1.2.42.'
3. Official History, Vol. II, p. 169.
4. Ibid., p. 167.
5. Ibid., p. 170.
6. Ibid.
7. Official History, Vol. II, p. 171.
8. Ibid., p. 172.
9. Ibid., p. 174.
10. Kahn, *Seizing the Enigma*, p. 183.
11. Ibid.
12. Official History, Vol. II, p. 175.
13. Ibid., p. 176.
14. Ibid., p. 175.
15. Ibid., p. 176.
16. Ibid.

17. The famous letter is given in full in the Official History, Vol. II, Appendix 3, pp. 655–7.
18. But a completely new wheel would have meant a bigger machine – not suitable to fit existing shipboard dimensions. The new wheel, therefore, was a narrow or 'thin' design, placed next to a new thin reversing wheel or drum.

# Chapter 12

# DEFEAT FOR THE U-BOATS

To add to the U-boat blackout which engulfed Hut Eight for the rest of 1942 – with the Admiralty thrown back on traditional methods such as direction-finding[1] and aerial reconnaissance – were a further series of misfortunes. The US now at war, American destroyers were re-called from Atlantic escort duty for service in the Pacific. British destroyers were required to escort convoys to the Mediterranean and later, the large seaborne Operation Torch, the Allied landings in North Africa, again robbed the Atlantic convoys of much-needed escort vessels.

To add to the list of 'fortunes', or rather, misfortunes, of war, afflicting the Allies in the Atlantic, was the singularly unfortunate fact that the loss of the Ultra intelligence coincided with the breaking, by the *B-Dienst*, of the convoy cipher, which was used jointly by Britain, Canada and the US, and to which we shall refer again. The combined effect of these two factors coupled with increasing numbers of U-boats, led directly to the enemy clearly gaining the upper hand by the end of the year. Although convoy escorts were bigger and better, their equipment and tactics much improved, and increasing air patrols had pushed the U-boat packs into the mid-Atlantic, there was no British or American aircraft made available that would cover the 'black hole' in the middle. In 1942 a large part of the Atlantic was covered by extended air activity from airfields in Northern Ireland, Newfoundland and Iceland. The gap in the middle, about 600 miles, stretched from Greenland to the Azores. Here the wolf-packs congregated.

Had Ultra still been available, it is almost certain that, by matching enemy intelligence received with the actions of the U-boat packs, the Admiralty could have been given proof that both their ciphers were being read. Eventually, in the spring of 1943, with Ultra restored, this is what happened.

Meanwhile, there were two urgent problems for the Allies in the Atlantic. Immediately, that of supplying Britain's wartime needs; then, for the slightly longer-term goal of a final assault on 'Fortress Europe', which presupposed a huge build-up based in Britain, the Atlantic would have to be swept clean. But the Atlantic was fast becoming the Achilles heel of the entire war effort – 1942 had seen the balance of war turn in favour of the Allies, but more ships had been sunk during the year than had been built.

The United States, for all its large navy, was inexperienced in modern warfare, and already infected with the arrogance of a 'great power', ignored the advice of its ally about forming merchant ships into convoys, and chose to disregard a warning from the British (via BP) that fifteen U-boats were lurking off their coast in December 1941. Theirs was going to be a hard lesson. For the first six months of 1942 the U-boats operating off the American coast had what they called their 'happy time', with ships being sunk in broad daylight, sometimes in full view of holidaymakers at coastal resorts where the lights could not be turned off at night because it would be 'bad for trade'. Over one million tons were sunk off the US east coast in the first three months of 1942.

Meanwhile the effect of the loss of information on the whereabouts of U-boats was becoming increasingly serious month by month as the U-boat fleet steadily increased in size. In one action, in March 1942, U-boats caught two convoys at the same time, sinking twenty-one out of ninety-eight vessels for the loss of just one U-boat. Added to the blackout at Bletchley Park, American ineptitude and withdrawal of naval escorts, was the awesome fact that from the beginning of the year Naval Cipher No. 3, the convoy cipher, was being read by the enemy. At this time *B-Dienst* were producing about 2,000 decodes a month. By December, they were reading 80 per cent of messages intercepted; up to 10 per cent of these in time to be tactically useful. No wonder that every suggestion on the German side that the British were reading their ciphers was always dismissed. How could anyone whose ciphers were being broken with the regularity of the British Admiralty's be clever enough to read the Enigma?

### 'the War can be lost unless . . .'

Despite warnings that their own signals were insecure, the Admiralty tended to see only BP's failure. On 22 November 1942, the OIC asked BP Naval Section to pay 'a little more attention' to the unbroken Shark key – but this schoolmasterish opening was followed by a more passionate plea, 'the one campaign [that against the U-boats] which Bletchley Park are not at present influencing to any marked extent – and it is the only one in which the war can be lost unless BP *do* help.'[2]

Although the Admiralty resisted suggestions that the enemy might be reading their ciphers, and cited in their defence the complete surprise achieved by the Torch landings in North Africa as evidence to the contrary, they nonetheless decided to encipher their system indicators in December 1942. Actions speak louder than words. The November losses had been the worst so far and only two U-boats sunk. Clearly, the Battle of the Atlantic was being lost and the change to the system indicators may look like an act of desperation. The move actually gave them two months' respite, *B-Dienst* not breaking the new encipherment until the following February. This coincided with the rebirth of Hut Eight, also in December, and together, these factors must have accounted for the much reduced losses in January.

Gradually, as bitter experience concentrated minds, an Anti-U-boat Committee was formed with boffins from both sides of the ocean and with Churchill as chairman. This, like so much Allied endeavour in the Second World War, was only just in time. In 1940 it had been said that if the U-boat fleet, then numbering about sixty, were ever trebled, Britain would be in real danger. Now the fleet had grown to ninety at the beginning of 1942, and was to grow to over 200 towards the end of the year, of which one hundred were known to be at sea in October. As though all this were not bad enough, U-boat Command had developed U-tankers – large (2,000-ton) submarines, which could refuel, rearm and restock U-boats in out-of-the-way locations, extending their operational period from around forty-five days to about sixty-five days for a Type IX U-boat. The Admiralty were reluctant to believe it, as the effective size of the U-boat force was thus dramatically increased. However the morale and physical condition of the submarine crews began to suffer.

Even if BP had been functioning well and supplying OIC with fairly current U-boat intelligence, re-routeing would have become very difficult towards the end of that fateful year. There were just too many U-boats. What was urgently needed was direct action, a counter-offensive using the weapons of modern warfare. Fortunately, a number of developments were in train, and these were now brought forward. They included centimetric radar which showed an outline shape, e.g. of a U-boat or coastline, instead of blips on a screen, the Leigh light, which enabled aircraft to spot a submarine on the surface at night, new Asdic equipment for detecting submerged boats, and new offensive weapons, such as better depth charges,[3] and more reconnaissance aircraft, including the new very-long-range B24 bomber, which could cover the mid-Atlantic gap.

## Light at the end of the Med.

Then came another change in the fortunes of war. This time a stroke of sheer luck which might be an answer to the Admiralty's prayer. On 30 October 1942, a Sunderland flying boat reported a radar contact, 'possibly a sub', in the eastern Mediterranean between Port Said and Tel Aviv. Four destroyers were ordered to search the area. Among them was HMS *Petard*, under Lieutenant Commander Thornton, whose burning ambition to capture a U-boat made him the right man for the job. The hunt continued for fifteen hours, the destroyers never losing the scent. After many attacks, and despite seeing oil on the surface, no contact was made. The boat, U-559, was one of those transferred to the Mediterranean in the autumn of 1941, and now on its tenth voyage with a record of success. Eventually, cross bearings of Asdic contacts were obtained, but one of the *Petard*'s torpedomen sent word to Thornton that he thought the sub was lying below 500 feet, the maximum depth, at that time, for Royal Navy depth charges, a fact probably known to U-boat commanders. He asked for permission to 'soap up' the next charge. By stuffing soap into the holes of the depth charge, the pressure would build up more slowly, and the charge sink deeper, before exploding. The dodge worked, the U-boat moved and contact was re-established. Attacks continued for over three hours until just after 22.00 the *Dulverton* and the *Petard* obtained matching ranges and bearings, and the crew felt the end must be near. Thornton attacked once more, this time scoring a direct hit which holed the bow and stoved in the plates on the starboard quarter. The air having become unbreathable, the commander raised the U-boat. The crew had counted 288 explosions, and very thankful that they had not gone to the bottom, abandoned ship.

Thornton sent a well-rehearsed boarding party, and although the vessel was very badly damaged and taking on water, they managed to remove documents and equipment. As the last two members of the boarding party were struggling to leave, the boat went down suddenly, taking Lieutenant Fasson and Able-Seaman Grazier with it. (Both were awarded the George Cross posthumously.) The documents recovered were exactly what Hut Eight needed – the second edition of the Short Weather Cipher book and the Short Signal Book.

## An enemy blunder

With the November 1942 sinkings the worst ever, Britain's imports of food and raw materials again in danger, the Royal Navy itself down to two months' supply of fuel oil, the entire political and military establishment were getting jumpy and bearing down on the Admiralty. They, in turn, were hoping that Bletchley could produce another miracle, when in reality, all that could overcome such an armada of U-boats as were now operating, would be downright naval and air action, using forces and resources comparable to those of the enemy. But the capture of the U-559 looked like 'manna from heaven', and some admirals assumed salvation was at hand judging by their messages to Washington.

Although the newly-acquired Short Weather and Short Signal books gave them cribs, Hut Eight lacked four-wheel, high-speed Bombes, and it might take several weeks for their existing three-wheel Bombes to work through the wheel settings in order to cope with just one day's traffic (as the Doenitz 'promotion signal' had exemplified). But here they were saved by an enemy blunder – one of those mistakes to which code-making is prone – only this time it was the super-cautious, meticulous U-boat Command signals staff who had not thought through the new procedure.

Most U-boat Enigma signals used either the Short Weather Cipher or the Short Signal Book – sighting and position reports, situation reports, estimated time of return. But the Short Weather Cipher book only gave three-letter settings, so the fourth wheel was set in a 'neutral' position effectively doing away with the advantage of the additional wheel. This would not have been decisive if all other enciphered messages had produced four-wheel darkness, but the Hut Eight boffins found, to their complete astonishment, that Enigma ciphers using the Short Signal Book – the bulk of the traffic – were enciphered in the same way, effectively as though it were the old three-wheel machine! The boffins now needed to work through twenty-six additional possibilities for the fourth wheel, rather than the fearful number that would otherwise have been the case. It took Hut Eight three weeks of arduous testing to discover that three and not four wheels were used.

On 13 December, the first Shark key message to be deciphered indicated the presence of fifteen U-boats.[4] Re-routeing was once more attempted, the figures for losses in January falling well below the very high figures of the previous two months (including November, when the fatal 800,000 tons was exceeded for the third and last time). However, the Enigma was being read, but with delays, so that the Tracking Room's picture of the U-boat situation was 'far from perfect', as the Official History admits. It goes on to say that 'in partnership with . . . the US Navy Department, . . . it (BP) steadily completed its mastery over the Shark settings,' and this was accomplished by August 1943, after which daily success was assured until the end of the War. 'During the first half of 1943, however, while the traffic was read with delays that were sometimes less than 24 hours, and rarely exceeded 72 hours except on days when the settings proved to be unusually stubborn or intractable, such days, unfortunately, were not uncommon.'[5] Perhaps a reasonable decipherment of this message might read, 'Delays of 72 hours or more were fairly common.' And three days was too late to be of operational value in the rapidly-moving convoy battles then raging in the Atlantic. By the time news was received that the U-boats were to proceed to new positions, it would be too late to divert convoys.

## No fixed address . . .

Naval Section's problems did not come singly. One piece of information, more than any other, needed by the Tracking Room was the precise location of the U-boats. Without it, re-routeing would not often have been possible. The old problem of the 'address book' system of disguising positions at sea – first introduced by U-boat Command in late 1941, and not solved when darkness overtook BP on 1 February 1942 – was found to be still in use when deciphering was resumed in

December 1942. Naval Section and the OIC Tracking Room had to piece together scraps of information from a variety of sources in order to determine the position of the boats. These included sighting reports from Allied ships and aircraft, direction-finding, sometimes Radio Finger-Printing, a technique for studying the characteristics of wireless transmitters, and keeping records of Morse-key characteristics, the individual keying style, or 'fist', of particular wireless operators. The worst feature of the 'address book' was that the notional 'name and address' could be changed at any time and so bring in a new method of recording a position on the naval grid. Usually, a solution was found, but again, not without delay and, occasionally error, especially when a new 'address' was introduced.

Then in March 1943, the Short Weather Cipher, so recently captured from U-559, was rendered obsolete by the introduction of a third edition, and this caused deciphering to be delayed but only for ten days. The new edition still required the Enigma machine to be used as if it were a three-wheel machine, the fourth wheel remaining in a 'neutral' position. This was because the U-boats transmitted their weather reports 'at random', with no address, just a coded two-letter signature – and the shore stations which received these reports were not equipped with the four-wheel Enigma.

Happily, the Short Signal Book (also taken from U-559), which accounted for most of the traffic, remained in force. This tended to compensate, at least for the time being, for the loss of the weather signals, especially as the convoy battles, now reaching their peak, produced a copious supply of these short signals. But it is worth recalling that they were literally of very short duration, designed expressly to keep direction-finders and code-breakers at bay, so that the problem of feeding the Bombes with a reasonably accurate crib required a good deal of meticulously detailed investigation and detective work – and it had to be done quickly. Fortunately, by then Bletchley had some sixty Bombes. But they had lost those weather recipherments on which they had so heavily relied. By February, *B-Dienst* had regained its mastery over the convoy cipher, and combined with the temporary disappearance of Ultra intelligence, the big increase in U-boat strength – sixty-six in the north Atlantic alone, production having reached almost one a day – and a doubling in the number of convoy sailings (over February), led directly to the convoy battles of March when Doenitz had his greatest success. There was also continuing very bad weather which restricted air cover and escorts were still in short supply. Of all the factors involved, there is no doubt at all that *B-Dienst*'s steady stream of convoy movement intelligence to the U-boat Command was what mattered most. In early March all convoys were sighted and during the month forty-two ships were lost in the North Atlantic including the biggest shipping disaster of the War when two ill-fated convoys HX229 and SC 122 ran into two lines of U-boats over forty strong. About two dozen ships and 360 men went down for the loss of just one U-boat. What gave U-boat Command the upper hand was that, even when evasive routeing was attempted, the *B-Dienst* quickly deciphered the diversion, and with advance warning, U-boat Command, which exerted very close control, could deploy and redeploy its forces to the best advantage. This meant that the intense, round-the-clock, combined work of BP Naval Section and the OIC Tracking Room, was nullified. The Admiralty had now been given proof that their ciphers were being broken, but their best efforts could not replace Naval Cipher No. 3 before June, two years after the creaking machinery (both Admiralty and GC&CS) had been set in motion.

The Allies found themselves in a position not unlike that of the enemy in the autumn of 1941, when the 'exigencies of the situation' had compelled them temporarily to disperse the U-boat fleet away from the shipping routes of the North Atlantic. In 1942 escort vessels were needed by the Allies to accompany convoys to the Arctic, and for the big Torch operation in November; the landings in North Africa and the subsequent Tunisian campaign. As it happened, this also affected U-boat Command, as Doenitz was obliged by his superiors to attack the south-bound convoys, which he did, though with conspicuous lack of success. This diversion of U-boats may be another factor in accounting for the much improved shipping results in January – twenty-nine ships lost, just below one a day for the first time for a year. The Torch operation was, in size and preparation, something of an overkill. But it had to succeed – the Allies wanted the Germans and Italians out of North Africa. The convoy escorts included support groups with escort carriers. These support groups were intended to 'search (for) and destroy' enemy submarines. Combined with aircraft from the carrier they could be very effective. Escort vessels now routinely carried high-frequency direction-finding equipment, and increasingly, ships and aircraft were being equipped with the new centimetric radar.[6] Very effective at short range, the new radar, with a 360° sweep, could create a 'screen' around the convoy at night, but was affected by bad weather. Aircraft were painted white, the more difficult to be seen from below, and flew higher, the better to detect submerged U-boats.

## Victory snatched from the jaws of defeat

At the Casablanca Conference in January 1943, with D-Day now only eighteen months away, the Atlantic was at long last accorded priority by the Allied powers, so that by late March support groups had been formed, and escort carriers made available, together with more aircraft; above all, about twenty very-long-range bombers that could bridge the 'Greenland gap' were allocated to the Royal Canadian Air Force. And now speed was of the essence, the invasion of Sicily (with 160,000 men) was scheduled for 10 July.

By the end of March the tide had begun to turn. New features began to appear, larger numbers of U-boats yet fewer sinkings. A decline in the morale of U-boat captains was becoming apparent – a consequence both of their lack of experience and of increased air attack. In place of his old exhortations to 'kill, kill, kill!' Bletchley was now reading peevish admonitions from Doenitz about such poor results from so many boats, and lack of the 'warrior hunter' spirit. The ratio of ships lost to U-boats destroyed was gradually approaching one to one.

Doenitz was obliged to call off one action in which he lost six boats. A series of running battles followed in which the U-boats sustained further losses until on 24 May, when the attacks on convoys SC 130 and HX 239 had resulted in the loss of eight boats with no ships sunk, Doenitz ordered a 'temporary withdrawal' to areas where there is 'less danger from aircraft'. Doenitz recorded in his official war diary for May that recently the 'sinking of 10,000 tons was paid for by the loss of one U-boat', whereas prior to that, 'one boat was lost for the sinking of about 100,000 tons', revealing one of the most rapid reversals in the history of the War – from near victory to humiliating defeat in eight weeks! Nearly one hundred U-boats were lost in the first five months of 1943. Doenitz, now Grand Admiral, Commander-in-Chief of Hitler's entire navy, described these losses as 'unbearable', and never returned to the Atlantic in such force. BP had deciphered a telegram from the Japanese Ambassador in Berlin, reporting that, 'Hitler was complaining that because the war had started too soon, "we have been unable to dominate the seas." '[7] Who could have started the War?

133

# Air power makes cowards of us all

In the mopping-up operations that took place in the ensuing three months, American aircraft-carrier planes guided by Ultra intelligence and by direction-finding, sank five U-boat supply tankers, forcing Doenitz to bring his operations in mid-Atlantic to an end sooner than expected. This fruitful co-operation between BP and the US Navy resulted in a further thirteen U-boats being sunk in July and August after being hunted down in vast stretches of ocean, and putting paid to a new offensive armed with acoustic homing torpedoes. Clearly, air power sounded the death-knell of the submarines, provided of course, the aircraft knew where to find them.

What air power did, as Doenitz complained, was not only deprive the U-boat of its chief asset, invisibility, but when surfaced, drove it under-water, where, with a much reduced speed, it could not keep up with the convoy. Doenitz complained of air power when he stood trial for war crimes at Nuremberg after the War. What he did not mention was that at the height of the Battle of the Atlantic, air power was breaking the morale of his U-boat commanders, a factor noted by the Tracking Room during the final battles, when those who had broken the lives of so many were themselves turning into timorous cowards. And what he must have strongly suspected, was that code-breakers telling the aircraft where to find the submarines was the winning combination.

It is difficult to assess the part played by BP Naval Section and Hut Eight in the final phase of the Battle of the Atlantic. As we have seen, the rebirth of Hut Eight on 13 December 1942 coincided very fortu-nately with the new Admiralty cipher changes on 15 December which set the *B-Dienst* back by two whole months at a critical time. The intelli-gence thus gained, although subject to delays, and the convoy diversions made possible, must have reduced Allied shipping losses in January and perhaps February.

The Official History, although insisting on a key role for Naval Section and OIC in the Battle, can blow cold as well as hot. 'But the battle which was fought in the Atlantic between December 1942 and May 1943 was the most prolonged and complex battle in the history of naval warfare, and when its outcome clearly hinged on many factors it is not easy to establish the extent to which it was influenced by the Allied decryption [deciphering] of the signals of the U-boat Command.'[8] The

History acknowledges that delays in deciphering could reduce its effectiveness.

> A convoy could at best cover 240 miles in 24 hours, whereas the U-boats might cover between 320 and 370 miles in the same period. A delay of as much as three days . . . could thus mean that the intelligence was received too late to be of use in diverting convoys. Moreover, it became increasingly likely that this would be so throughout the period from December 1942 to May 1943.[9]

This was because of the increase in numbers of U-boats and of those operating on the northern convoy routes. Not only was there no Enigma traffic broken between 19 and 25 December, but 'By 17 February, for example, the settings had not been broken for ten days in January, and no traffic had been read since 10 February. And between 10 March and end of June the settings for a further 22 days were either not broken at all or broken only after a long delay.'[10] Herculean efforts enabled Hut Eight to survive without their staple, the Short Weather Cipher, which, as we saw earlier, had gone into a new edition. But they had made their contingency plans, and some evasive routeing continued, sporadically, with limited success, attempts frequently frustrated by *B-Dienst*'s very quick reading of the convoy cipher, and of course, the sheer numbers of U-boats. (rising to 240 in May, of which over sixty were tactically deployed across the eastbound convoy routes of the North Atlantic).

Not only did the depredations of the *B-Dienst* and the rapidly increasing size of the U-boat fleet militate against BP's work, but the very increase in the number of convoy sailings (the pace of the war accelerating) demanded even quicker solutions from Hut Eight, demands that were just not possible to meet. The history points out that nearly half the convoys sailing between January and May escaped detection by U-boats, and some of this they say, must be attributable to deciphering the Enigma.

In considering what help deciphering the Enigma gave the Allied escort and support forces in the final battles of April and May, the History has this to say, 'From the beginning of 1943 *the all but continuous reading of the Shark traffic* [author's italics] had yielded a vast amount of information about the equipment and the characteristics of the U-boats, including the endurance, fuel consumption and speed of

135

the various types.'[11] After more in this vein, we get, 'As for the extent to which the intelligence assisted the Allied escorts and support forces in the Atlantic, this is a matter for surmise.'[12]

In its conclusions the History comments, 'Between February and June, 1943 the battle of the Atlantic hinged to no small extent on the changing fortunes of a continuing trial of [code-making] and [code-breaking] resourcefulness between the B-Dienst and the Allies.'[13] The editors eventually acknowledge that there was more to the battle than the intelligence contest.

> But if the battle in the north Atlantic was more than a duel between the cryptanalysts [code-breakers] and intelligence staffs of the two sides . . . one conclusion still stands out when its course is reviewed up to the end of March 1943. But for the contribution of the Enigma to evasive routeing, the planned mass assaults of the U-boats would have achieved in January and February 1943, the enormous success that they secured only in March.[14]

The History may huff and puff but, like the previous suggestion that as nearly half the convoys between January and May escaped detection, some of which must be due to Ultra, this claim can neither be proved nor disproved. It might just as easily be pointed out that two convoys out of three escaped detection in August and September 1942, when Hut Eight was still in the dark. There are many variables. The low rate of sinkings in January and partly in February could, to a large extent, be attributed to the Admiralty deciding to encipher their indicators in mid-December 1942, which put *B-Dienst* out of action for two months; and the increase in February to fifty ships lost (from the low January figure of twenty-nine) could be said to be the result of *B-Dienst* having recovered its mastery over the convoy cipher in the middle of that month. Furthermore, a number of U-boats had to be detached to try and attack the southbound Torch convoys. Part of the great enemy success in March, it may be argued, was due not only to the ever-increasing numbers of U-boats, but the increased number of convoys as well; more hunters and more prey.

The stark fact was that even convoys under strong escort were being ambushed and badly mauled. Imports into Britain in January 1943, were half those of January 1941. Even before the disasters of March, when ninety-seven vessels were sunk, three-quarters of them in convoy, it was obvious that the enemy had gained the upper hand. The U-boat building programme was rapidly filling the Atlantic, and *B-Dienst* was giving ten to twenty hours advance notice of convoy movements and diversions – both the sea war and the intelligence war were very clearly being lost. For all the frantic endeavour on the part of Huts Eight and Four and the OIC, their efforts were simply marginalized by events.

Then the Allies, at the eleventh hour, marshal a formidable array of the engines of modern warfare, and within eight weeks the enemy has been put to flight; in May he loses forty-one submarines in exchange for a handful of merchant ships, and withdraws – the 'pond' has been swept clean.

The claim, made in some war histories, that 'Ultra' or breaking the Shark key at the end of 1942, was the 'key factor' in the British victory, will not bear examination.

Marc Milner, a naval historian, concludes that 'the elimination of the air gap would have defeated the wolf-packs without Ultra, although special intelligence allowed it to happen faster and with more telling effect. It was air power that forced submarines to operate fully submerged as a normal mode.'[15] That means failing to keep up with all but the slowest convoys, and finding it difficult to receive wireless transmissions except at night, thus depriving Doenitz of that close control essential to his wolf-pack system.

## Notes

1. Accuracy of direction-finding depended on weather conditions at sea, and even very good operators could err by (+/-) 3°. With six bearings it was possible to locate a submarine to within twenty-five miles. High frequency D/F equipment increasingly carried aboard escort vessels, could be more accurate.
2. Official History, Vol. II, p. 548.
3. Coastal Command aircraft were equipped with the 250-lb depth charge – devastating to U-boats
4. Alan Turing, sometimes credited with having 'solved' the Shark key, had sailed for the US on 7 November, before the arrival of the vital documents.
5. Official History, Vol. II, p. 552.
6. 9.7cm; previous wavelength 1.5m – the old one still being vainly monitored by the U-boats.
7. Official History, Vol. II, p. 572.
8. Ibid., p. 549.

9. Ibid., pp. 552–3.
10. Ibid., p 552.
11. Ibid., p. 556.
12. Ibid., p. 567.
13. Ibid., p. 554.
14. Ibid., p. 556.
15. *The Oxford Companion to the Second World War* (Oxford, OUP, 1995), p. 68.

# Chapter 13

# COLOSSUS AND TUNNY –
# THE BIG FISH

## . . . Miracles Take a Little Longer!

By 1944, there may have been 50,000 Enigma machines in use in the German armed forces. Doubts about the security of the Enigma system, regarded in the early years as totally impregnable, were raised, not for the first time, and there was a high-level conference on the subject, but it failed to make any radical changes.

Generally, Enigma was used by the three services for operational purposes, at the headquarters level of armies, of corps and of divisions (and of their air force equivalents), although the U-boat Command used it extensively for daily tactical purposes. Enigma was not used at the level of army groups[1] or for communications at the very highest level, such as the High Command in Berlin to commanders-in-chief in particular theatres of war. Prior to 1941 and the rapid German expansion into southern and eastern Europe, such communications would have been by land-line, probably teleprinter or scrambler telephone. But as the new Nazi empire spread, recourse was had to a new form of secret wireless transmission, regarded as so secure that it could eventually be used for such highly sensitive traffic as that between the OKW[2] (High Command) and von Rundstedt, Commander-in-Chief, West, during the Allied invasion of western Europe, and occasionally from Hitler to his generals.

During the 1930s teleprinters had come into general use, and messages could be sent using the five-digit International (Baudot-Murray) Teleprinter code instead of Morse code. Although the teleprinter would automatically 'encode' the message (and 'decode' it at the other end), this was simply to enable the message to be sent quickly over the line (as a sequence of electrical pulses), and also allow equipment made by different manufacturers to be used for sending and receiving. It was certainly not a secret code. This universal acceptance by manufacturers and users, governments, post offices, and so on, as we shall see, was all to the good.

The 'alphabet' of the code had thirty-two symbols which could be made to represent twenty-six letters of the alphabet (plus six more for typewriter operations, line-feed, carriage return, etc.) using five-hole paper tape. The patterns of holes produced by operating the keyboard would be converted into pulses and sent by 'line' (as in telephone line) or by wireless transmitter 'over the air'. At the receiving end the pulses would be turned back into plaintext and printed out on paper tape which could then be cut up and pasted, e.g. on to standard telegram forms. Some readers may have seen a teleprinted telegram – once used for sending urgent messages.

## Twelve wheels in all

From teleprinters it was not a very big step for the Germans to arrive at the notion that this pattern of pulses could be disguised by 'adding' a second teleprinter tape, a 'key' tape, which would have the effect of changing the pattern of the first tape.[3] The method used for this purpose was a cipher machine (attached to the teleprinter) using revolving wheels with spring-loaded teeth around the circumference which could be left in place or folded away. These wheels and the pattern of teeth adopted were used for the actual disguising of the tele-printer signal elements, each of the five digits being passed through one of a set of five coding wheels, and then through a second set of five, which produced the enciphered character that was then put 'on line' to be deciphered by a similar machine at the other end, creating an auto-matic enciphering, transmission and deciphering process.[4] Exactly how the original signal elements would be processed by the machine would depend on how it was set up (shades of Enigma). The coding wheels – twelve in all – had varying numbers of teeth which were set to a predetermined pattern, according to the cipher clerk's instructions, which could mean that from time to time he would have to adjust as many as 501 teeth.

# 'Fish'

The wheels themselves could be revolved independently according to the instructions for given starting positions which had to be set up before each transmission.[5] This high-speed, automatically enciphered, non-Morse traffic,[6] beamed by wireless between two points (called a link), was first intercepted in Britain, with considerable difficulty, in 1940. Then in 1941 Bletchley managed to break the experimental link between Athens and Vienna using 'hand methods'. This success, while the system was still in the experimental stage, was a great advantage, and enabled BP to keep up with changes to the system made by the enemy. What the code-breakers had to do was to work out the patterns of the teeth, and then the wheel starting positions for all twelve wheels of the German machine. The task was not only immensely difficult but very tedious as well as labour and time-consuming, and could not hope to deal with more than a proportion of the traffic which began to increase markedly from the middle of 1942 – as the war became more intense. Considering the extreme complexity of these transmissions, it was a near-miracle that anything was achieved at all!

All of this non-Morse traffic was given the general cover-name 'Fish' at BP. Confusingly, this derives from '*Sägefisch*' (sawfish), the enemy code-name for the Luftwaffe's teleprinter cipher machine (Siemens T52), which Bletchley decided *not* to attack. Very wisely, BP had determined to concentrate its resources entirely against the army machine (Lorenz SZ40/42), which BP code-named 'Tunny', as there was adequate intelligence about the Air Force from Enigma sources. The army Enigma ciphers were generally more difficult than those of the Air Force as they had better trained men and were more guarded in what was sent over the air, although the naval ciphers were by far the most difficult. In any case, the coming invasion of Europe would be a predominantly military campaign. While 'Fish' was used as a general term, the word 'Tunny' could describe: a) the German army machine, b) the traffic produced by this machine, and c) the British-built equivalent machine.

## A colossal blunder!

The enemy cipher machine against which, from 1942, BP increasingly pitted its brains and resources, was the Lorenz SZ 40/42

*Schlüsselzusatz*[7] (cipher attachment, i.e. attached to a standard Lorenz teleprinter) which was used by the German military for top-level communication, and was not captured until the very end of the War.

The first miracle of code-breaking was started off as a result of an enemy blunder. In 1941 a German cipher clerk had sent out the same long message twice, each time enciphered by the same key, which should never happen. Someone at Bletchley, who should have had a knighthood, had guessed what had happened, and a comparison of the two enabled Colonel Tiltman to recover both key and original plaintext.

> With a machine designed for complete security, it should have proved impossible to make any further progress. The sequence of Key thus elucidated should have appeared to be random, without any discernible pattern. But it was not. The decisive observation was made by W.T. Tutte, a young Cambridge chemist turned mathematician. This was the breakthrough equivalent to what the Poles had achieved with the Enigma in 1932.[8]

In fact, Tutte, 'after a few months, was able to deduce the entire structure of the Tunny machine including the lengths (numbers of teeth) of all the wheels'.[9] This surely deserves a peerage, except that further miracles were in the pipeline and Bletchley (and Dollis Hill) were to yield an entire aristocracy of the talents.

Following Bill Tutte's breakthrough, a new section was of course established at Bletchley to exploit the discovery. This was set up in 1942 under Major Tester (who had a wide knowledge of German and Germany) and in the usual parlance became the 'Testery'.[10] Among those who worked there were: Roy Jenkins (later Chancellor of the Exchequer), Peter Benenson (who founded Amnesty International), Peter Hilton (later Professor of Mathematics at New York State University), W.T. Tutte, Donald Michie (later Professor of Machine Intelligence at Edinburgh University) and M.H.A. ('Max') Newman (later Professor of Mathematics at Manchester University). They continued to achieve success using hand methods and by early 1943 a proportion of the Tunny traffic was being read without undue delay. But only a proportion. Before that however, Newman, a leading Cambridge mathematician, saw that some of the work of the Testery could be done by machinery and persuaded Commander Travis of the wisdom of this.

# Electronic 'wizards'

In the autumn of 1942 contact with Dollis Hill[11] was renewed and C.E. Wynn-Williams, an inventive Cambridge physicist with previous experience of electronics, who had been working on radar at TRE,[12] was asked to design a machine to help solve the Fish traffic. He was assisted by four members of the Physics Group at Dollis Hill who designed and engineered a 'tape reader', an optical scanning system which, as the punched paper tape went past, sent light pulses to an array of photoelectric cells. (They were probably not told the purpose of the project.) The machine, with a pair of long paper tapes driven over pulley wheels soaring toward the ceiling, was soon dubbed 'Heath-Robinson' or simply 'Robinson'. After the tape patterns had been read by the photoelectric cells, the internal parts of the machine, including some 'two dozen valves', could do the very rapid counting and comparison required. It was built by Post Office engineers under Tommy Flowers and by April 1943 was installed in Hut F where a new section led by Max Newman had been set up (the 'Newmanry'). To begin with, this was intended to complement the work of the Testery by mechanizing some of their heavy mathematical burden. To assist Newman, Jack Good was transferred from Hut Eight (the Battle of the Atlantic being nearly over) and Donald Michie from the Testery. Together, they formed a very good partnership.

Technically, the Bombe had been designed to make maximum use of electro-magnetic relays for multiple switching operations. If the Fish traffic were ever to be conquered in a comprehensive fashion, as so much Enigma traffic had been, the truly 'tremendously large number' of possibilities involved in deciphering a single Fish message, meant that something entirely new and far faster than relay-based machinery was required. An electronic valve – as had been shown as early as 1919 – could be used for switching purposes, and what is more, it could do so in one millionth of a second.

# Thousands of valves!

In the late 1930s and early 1940s, however, this was still a very novel idea, the valve being associated principally with wireless equipment, especially as a valve amplifier. They were also considered liable to failure and they gave out a good deal of heat.

The Heath-Robinson project was beset with problems. 'The main weakness of the design was the driving of the tapes partly by their sprocket holes at about a hundred times the speed of the tapes in normal teleprinter usage. This would cause these holes to stretch and the tape to have a tendency to tear . . . Also, from time to time the machine would begin to smoke,' wrote Jack Good, who goes on to give other reasons why progress was slow. 'One trouble was that the best runs were not being made. Michie and I did research in the evenings on the statistics of plain language and wheel patterns, and that improved matters. Another problem was that mistakes were made in the manufacture of further key tapes.'[13] Sufficient improvement was then made for a much more sophisticated design to be considered. Although they were scarce, Wynn-Williams was not the only electronics boffin available. Tommy Flowers, a Post Office engineer, had worked on experimental valve switching since 1931 and had been involved in an experimental telephone toll dialling circuit which was working in 1935. Flowers suggested that some of their worst problems could be overcome if the key patterns were stored inside the machine, i.e. electronically. This would leave only the cipher tape which could be driven by pulleys alone. Internal storage, however, would involve a lot more electronics. Whereas 'Heath-Robinson' had employed 'perhaps two dozen', the new design would require about 1,500 valves! Wynn-Williams was very doubtful, but Newman agreed. This was to be 'Colossus I', built very secretly at Dollis Hill by a small team of engineers working under Tommy Flowers, including S.W. Broadhurst, W.W. Chandler and A.W.M. Coombs. No one else was allowed to see all the parts nor did anyone have an inkling of the purpose for which it was built.

## 'Leave them switched on!'

Work began in February 1943 (even before Robinson was finished). 'There were no drawings for many of the parts, only the designers' originals; there were no manuals, no accounts, nor questions asked about materials and labour consumed. In the laboratory the machine was assembled, wired and made to work in separate sections which did not come together until the machine was installed and working at Bletchley

144

in December 1943.'[14] After a few early problems Colossus worked very well, the doubts about the reliability of such large numbers of valves being scattered to the winds. Flowers knew something that Wynn-Williams may not have known. He knew that valves 'were reliable if the machine was left switched on all the time. I regard that as one of the great secrets of the war.'[15]

This is not only another incredible winning streak for Bletchley Park, but there is an almost uncanny parallel with the Bombe, when the BTM Co. at Letchworth were found to be the perfect partners for that project. On that occasion 'Doc' Keen at the factory had readily grasped the strange requirements and was able to facilitate construction. This time Tommy Flowers, the electronics 'wizard', had taken a major hand in the design and had come up with a novel development that had revolutionized the concept, rather as Welchman's 'diagonal board' had transformed Turing's original design.

Turning to Alan Turing, by the spring of 1943 he had just returned from a mission to the United States having left Hut Eight where he had led the fight against the U-boats. Turing had become a sort of general consultant – one of the few boffins at the Park to whom the 'need to know' rule did not apply. He was let into secret projects and his opinion often sought. There is no doubt that he was, to some extent, involved in the intensive work on Fish that went on in 1942. His biographer comments,

> One of the most important and general methods was developed by Alan on the basis of Tutte's work in the course of his months of work during 1942 on Fish. It became known as 'Turingismus'. A new Bletchley industry was sprouting up . . . But this was not to become Alan Turing's game, as naval Enigma had been. For one thing, he had not been the one to start it off. For another, it was someone else who took the step of mechanising its analysis. This person was Newman.[16]

Later, his biographer says,

> Alan knew all about these developments [Colossus] but declined the invitation to play a direct part. Newman built up an increasingly large and powerful group, drawing in the best talent from other huts and from the mathematical world outside. Alan moved in the opposite direction; he was not a Newman, skilled in overall direction . . . He had not fought to retain control of naval Enigma, but had retreated before Hugh Alexander's

organising power. If he had been quite a different person, he could now have made his position one of great influence, it being the time for sitting on co-ordinating committees . . . But he had no concern for finding a place in anything but scientific research itself.[17]

Although the War was giving scientists influence previously denied them, 'for Alan Turing the war had certainly brought new experiences and ideas, and the chance to do something. But it had given him no taste for organising other people, and it had left his axioms unchanged. A confirmed solitary, he wanted something of his own again.'[18]

When Alan Turing was in charge of Hut Eight it became clear that he conspicuously lacked the administrative skills necessary, and the BP management had to rely on Alexander, Turing's deputy – also a clever mathematician, but a capable organizer and good with people – in order to run this vitally important section efficiently.

The miracle of Colossus could be summed up in the word 'team-work', and it was not Turing's scene. Late in 1943 he left BP in order to develop a speech encipherment system.

In the early months of 1944 Michie and Good realized that they could make manual adjustments to Colossus I that would help speed up the wheel-breaking that was done in the Testery, as well as find the daily settings for the wheels that had been the original purpose of Colossus. If, at this time, the teeth-setting of the wheels was still done monthly – and not yet daily – the people in the Testery would still have some breathing space. Nevertheless, the volume of the Fish traffic had increased enormously, from only six links in mid-1943, to twenty-six links early in 1944. If there were a mitigating factor, it was that the messages were usually long ones, or rather, that each transmission contained a number of messages, and if there is one thing code-breakers like, it is ample material.

## And then . . . Mark II

The development of Colossus Mark II was then pushed ahead. There were several pressing reasons. Although the Testery and Newmanry between them had deciphered around 300 Fish transmissions a month during 1943, the volume, as mentioned, was outrunning their resources. The preparations for Operation Overlord, the Allied invasion of Europe, were well advanced, and information on this subject from

146

Enigma sources had been scarce. An even more urgent reason for the commissioning of Mark II so soon after Mark I had come into use, was that the enemy, doubtless growing more nervous at the increasing likelihood of an invasion, had decided to strengthen security even of Fish transmissions, although the risk would be seen, or said to be, from disloyalty and treachery; anything but admit to the possibility of British code-breaking! Nevertheless, the Testery was halted in its tracks for a time in February 1944, the burden falling on Mark I. The Good-Michie manual improvements would be automated in Mark II and all the work speeded up.

## World's first electronic computer

An order was placed with Dollis Hill in March 1944, for delivery of Colossus Mark II by 1 June (five days before D-Day). In March, the date for the invasion had not yet been decided, but it was a brilliant guess. Mark II would be five times faster;[19] it would incorporate considerable technical improvement and be much more flexible. The price they had to pay for all this was an increase to 2,500 valves – a colossal number. The time allowed was impossibly short, but it was built at breakneck speed, by the same team led by Tommy Flowers, probably working day and night, and was finished on time. It was the world's first electronic computer, albeit designed for a very specific purpose. As Jack Good remarked, 'Since the mid-1960s, if there is a laborious calculation to be done, everybody thinks of programming it for a computer; but the mid-1940s were not the mid-1960s.'[20]

To the Allied Commands, Fish intelligence had already proved itself a planning factor of the highest order. One of the most important of many important non-Morse links already broken was the link on the Russian front from the German High Command to Army Group South which gave, well in advance, immense detail of German preparations for the attack on the Kursk salient in July 1943, probably the most important battle on the whole Eastern Front, if not the entire war. Whether this information was supplied to the Russians is uncertain. About this time (May 1943) the link between Berlin and Kesselring, Hitler's Commander-in-Chief, South, in Rome, was first broken and continued to be broken. In March 1944, the most important Fish link of all was broken, that from the High Command in Berlin to von Rundstedt, Commander-in-Chief, West, which had opened two months earlier. This played a key role in detecting German plans to counter the invasion.

The Poles, we may now recall, and contrary to speculation on the subject, never did obtain a German military Enigma machine. From information supplied by the spy, Thilo-Schmidt, Marian Rejewski managed to deduce the wiring of the codewheels and from what they already knew – probably of the commercial version of the machine – simply built their own. It even had a different keyboard layout, but it worked.

As already mentioned, W.T. Tutte was able to deduce the 'entire structure of the Tunny machine, including the lengths of all the wheels', so it would have been possible for Bletchley to develop their own deciphering equipment.

Having, almost miraculously, derived the 'key' – the teeth patterns and wheel starting positions – a simulated Tunny machine would then be necessary, and the operator supplied with this information, so that the intercepted message tape could be fed into his correctly set up machine which would decipher the message.

Whatever machinery they already had, the decision was taken in March 1944, under the same pressures that gave rise to Colossus II, to build a simulated Tunny machine. As Fish traffic contained intelligence of the utmost sensitivity, and was 'probably worth thirty divisions' to the Allies, the manufacture would require a much higher degree of security than could be obtained in the normal type of factory or workshop. Once again the work was entrusted to Dollis Hill. But this was a Post Office research establishment that simply lacked the extensive machining facilities, etc. of an ordinary engineering factory. Ken Halton, one of the Tunny team, explains how the problem was overcome.

> The [British] Tunny machine performed the same function electrically as did the SZ42 [German Tunny] mechanically, but physically it did not resemble it in any way . . . It was certainly not a machine in the normal sense, but was made from a variety of the components used in the automatic and manual telephone exchanges of that time. Perhaps the most significant items to be simulated were the coding wheels of the SZ42. In Tunny [i.e. the British machine], their function was carried out by electrically driven switches in which an input wire could be connected to any one of twenty-five output wires in sequence. The output wires were made to behave as the teeth of the coding wheels.[21]

148

# Meccano . . . a new secret weapon!

Gil Hayward, an Intelligence Officer who was seconded to work on the design and construction of the Tunny machine with the Post Office engineers, continues the story:

> The Tunny design team was headed by Sid Broadhurst . . . and his concept of the German look-alike machine was based entirely on readily available standard Post Office parts such as 3,000 type relays and uniselectors. . . . all the development and construction work was carried out in one small laboratory . . . and mainly by the design team themselves. It was imperative that no one should know that the make-up of the SZ was known to us and . . . no formal drawings or circuit diagrams were ever made. Those necessary for the construction were done freehand . . . The beauty of Sid Broadhurst's design was that orders for our stores would give no hint as to the use to which they were being put . . . I privately cherished the idea of building an SZ with Meccano, using standard-sized sprockets with chains having links equal in number to the teeth on each rotor [wheel] . . . the notion of defeating the Germans with a Meccano model had a certain appeal. In the event our electro-mechanical models proved to be more flexible and easier to modify than the [real] SZ machine we were able to examine after the end of hostilities.[22]

Altogether, ten Mark II Colossus machines were built to help in the breaking of the Fish traffic, together with a number of Tunny machines for deciphering. Most were broken up at the end of the War for reasons which are still not clear.

Colossus was Bletchley's ultimate achievement. In reading enemy intelligence at the very highest operational and strategic level – the level of overall plans, strategic appreciations, future intentions, it was a true war-winning component. Unluckily, at the very outset, Mark II could not be put to use for long. The day before its due delivery date, 1 June 1944, Mark II was delivered, installed and working. By then, however, the Germans had become very jittery as Allied preparations for the landings could hardly be concealed, and the deception plan about the actual invasion areas had begun to wear thin. As in February, changes were made in the German Tunny procedure, only this time it was a major change which silenced BP from just a few days after the invasion of 6 June until October – the first four crucial months after Operation Overlord commenced. Very fortunately, the Berlin-von Rundstedt

(Commander-in-Chief, West) link had proved so valuable in the short time Bletchley had been reading it (March–early June) that the Allies had been able to adjust their plans and dispositions to meet the latest German preparations. This helped to ensure that the vital initial stages of the seaborne landings – the first the Allies had undertaken to be opposed by armoured divisions – were successful. That Bletchley was able to recover the lost traffic by the end of September, and was also able to read new links that had since come into operation, was due to having Mark II.

Colossus was all of a piece with the new scientific approach of the time. The highly gifted individual, a Turing or a Welchman, was no longer enough; Colossus was the work of a team. This time there were no Poles making a gift of vital equipment at a crucial moment, no captures of ships yielding essential documents. There was just one enemy blunder and the rest followed because of the way BP worked – the absence of sectional interests or serious friction – and its immense brain-power. But the right brains were selected or turned up, for the right jobs. Brilliant detection, design, electronics, engineering. Tiltman – Tutte – Newman – Wynn-Williams – Flowers – Good – Michie – Broadhurst, all vital links in the chain that eventually produced Mark II. This was a true 'aristocracy of the talents' in Thomas Jefferson's sense. Of this 'aristocracy', however, only Tommy Flowers received any official recognition, with the award of a modest MBE, although his contribution was outstanding. But then he was not a university man.

## Notes

1. Army groups – two or more armies; armies – two or more corps; corps – two or more divisions (12,500 to 15,000 men each).
2. *Oberkommando der Wehrmacht* (High Command).
3. For a mathematical explanation, see Good in Hinsley and Stripp, *Codebreakers*, p. 151 et seq.
4. These machines did not actually produce a paper 'key' tape, but to the code-breaker, the effect was the same. Enciphering and deciphering were reciprocal; there was no need to switch from one to the other.
5. This much-abbreviated account is from Halton in Hinsley and Stripp, *Codebreakers*, pp. 168 et seq.
6. Sometimes called radio teletype.
7. The generic term *'Geheimschreiber'* (secret writer) is often mistakenly applied to the SZ40/42.

8. Hodges, *Alan Turing*, p. 230.
9. Good in Hinsley and Stripp, *Codebreakers*, p. 161.
10. All deciphering has a 'mathematical' and a 'linguistic' side, although they often overlap; Fish traffic called for exceptional textual accuracy – hence the presence of some very 'wordy' people.
11. The Post Office Research Station, no stranger to 'secret projects', was situated in a secure location, at Dollis Hill, a London suburb.
12. TRE was the Telecommunications Research Establishment.
13. Hinsley and Stripp, *Codebreakers*., p. 162.
14. Hodges, Alan *Turing*, p. 268.
15. Good in Hinsley and Stripp, *Codebreakers*, p. 163.
16. Hodges, *Alan Turing*, p. 230.
17. Ibid., p. 268.
18. Ibid.
19. Two astounding features of Colossus II were: the photo-electric punched-tape reader which had previously operated at 5,000 characters per second, had now reached 25,000 c.p.s.! A clock-pulse had been introduced, years ahead of its time, to synchronize all aspects of the machine's operation.
20. Hinsley and Stripp, *Codebreakers*, p. 164.
21. Halton in Hinsley and Stripp, *Codebreakers*, p. 171.
22. Hayward in ibid., p. 176. These two contributions to *Codebreakers* provide further technical details.

# Chapter 14

# 1944 – THE INVASION
# OF EUROPE

## Allied Deception Plans

One of the main elements in weakening German opposition to the Allied invasion of Normandy was the creation of unreal threats. A peripheral threat to the German positions in Denmark and Norway was created by the simulation of seemingly large, but actually non-existent, forces in Scotland waiting to invade Scandinavia. Fabricated military encampments and airfields helped to deceive the enemy, especially as Allied air superiority prevented all but minimal aerial reconnaissance, although the mobile wireless stations, with their spoof messages, were real enough. In any case, as mentioned earlier, Hitler was in the grip of an obsessive delusion about Norway.

The main deception plan, 'Fortitude', was to pose a huge invasion threat by the creation of a large body of non-existent troops in East Anglia and south-east England, destined to go into the Pas de Calais area some three weeks after the invasion of Normandy which was made to appear as the feint, a mere subsidiary part of a wider strategy.

Deception, of course, is standard practice in warfare, and is expected, but in the case of this complex plan success was greatly assisted by the use of double agents and Ultra intelligence. BP had been reading the Enigma (and hand cipher) traffic of the *Abwehr*, the secret service of the German High Command, since 1941. British counter-intelligence had picked up all the *Abwehr* agents sent to Britain in the

152

second half of 1940 prior to a possible invasion, and had 'bent' or turned some of them into double agents who continued to send their 'reports' back to the *Abwehr*. These consisted of carefully blended mixtures of real, false and half-true information that was then closely monitored by deciphering *Abwehr* Enigma to see how much was being swallowed and which agents were still believed. In at least one case, a false report sent in the name of an agent who was still trusted by the *Abwehr*, caused the cancellation of an order to move the German 15th Army to Normandy.

The *Abwehr* Enigma machine differed from the military version. It had no plugboard (the No. 1 headache), which made deciphering considerably less difficult, but it had other complications, including a reversing wheel which revolved instead of the usual fixed wheel. Another great help to those struggling with *Abwehr* Enigma was that enemy operator discipline was poor.

## Breaking into 'Fortress Europe'

History books nowadays tend to assume that the success of the Allied invasion of Europe in June 1944 was a foregone conclusion. At the time, however, there was no such certainty, and one of the effects of Ultra intelligence was to inspire confidence when it may have been lacking. In the spring of 1944, the Allied invasion was imminent, and the enemy was greatly improving his preparations to meet it. Two strategies for dealing with the invasion were competing. Von Rundstedt, the Commander-in-Chief, West, was in favour of mobile forces, able to counter-attack at any point and deal with any threatened breakout from the beachheads. There were already static defence forces, often infantry, manning long stretches of the French coast, but Rommel felt that mining and barricading the beaches themselves, and attacking at the very moment of landing before any headway could be made, when the invaders would be at their most vulnerable, would be the most effective method. Rommel, recalling the successful Allied landings in North Africa, Sicily and Italy, was convinced that once a successful landing had been made, it would be extremely difficult to dislodge. (It could be argued that those landings were not opposed by armour; these certainly would be!) Hitler appeared to side with Rommel, and put him in charge – under von Rundstedt – of a group of armies (nominally forty-three divisions) stretching from Holland to Brittany. Whereas Stalin

153

eventually learned not to interfere in military operations, the German side suffered increasingly damaging interference from Hitler.

The Allied deception plans already mentioned had taken in the enemy for a time, but by the late spring of 1944, the German generals had begun to consider Normandy as the more likely invasion area. (Absence of mine-laying in the Seine Bay for example, was a good pointer.) Hitler, however, with a combination of over-caution and inability to make up his mind (hardly the qualities of a good general), still felt that even if the main thrust came in Normandy, an attack could still be launched in the Pas de Calais, and so kept nineteen divisions east of the Somme. Armoured reserves, on Hitler's orders, were kept outside Rommel's operational zone, and in fact, only eighteen divisions were in Normandy on the eve of the invasion. Hitler's insistence on scattering his forces resulted in those not in the right place when the invasion began, often being immobilized by the intense Allied air bombardment which wrecked a good deal of road and rail communication. One can begin to see how the old quip about 'the corporal turned field-marshal worth thirty divisions to the enemy' came about, as well as what was behind the plot against Hitler's life which occurred soon afterwards.

Although the enemy was beginning to guess if not the points, at least the area where the invasion would be attempted, a whole range of Allied measures, plus that superiority in the air which even denied the enemy reconnaissance over southern England, meant that they failed to detect the date of the invasion.

What the Allies needed to know was, first of all, where the enemy divisions were, and then the strength of such forces and of their reserves. And they most needed to know, if at all possible, whether the enemy would be able to concentrate fully-trained, or worse still, experienced troops, especially armoured divisions, and then be able to reinforce them sufficiently to prevent the beachheads being taken, and when taken, expanded. Estimates of this enemy strength, from a variety of intelligence sources, would determine the size and strength of the Allied assault force. In this, until the spring of 1944, the Allies had almost as much difficulty as the enemy had in deciding where and when the main thrust of the invasion would come.

Initial Allied estimates, dating from mid-1943, proved totally inadequate, and by early 1944, the proposed invasion force, including reinforcements, had been substantially increased and the invasion front lengthened. These changes were based on sources other than Ultra, which, given the static condition of many German forces in the west, and their little need to use wireless, was not surprising. But help was at hand. In January 1944, the Japanese Ambassador in Berlin was given a conducted tour of the western defences, and in his conscientious way, had sent a detailed report of what he had seen back to Tokyo by wireless, and this had been deciphered at Bletchley Park. Although some army and air force Enigma transmissions had begun to appear – mostly exercises but sufficient to enable Bletchley to break the new keys – the big Ultra breakthrough came when, at the end of March, the high-speed, non-Morse (Fish) link between Berlin and von Rundstedt was broken, probably with the aid of Colossus Mark I which had gone into service in January at about the same time as transmissions on the new link began.

Of some twenty-eight, mainly infantry, divisions manning the coastal defences, Ultra had identified about half, and in some cases located them as well. Many of these coastal defence formations had been in place before the Allied invasion threat became serious, and were second-grade troops, but one of those not located turned out to be 352nd Division, a better-quality field division, which happened to be on exercises very near the Omaha beach just before the invasion, the one landing where casualties were exceptionally heavy.[1] But this was accident and not design, and generally the enemy was taken completely by surprise by the invasion of 6 June, which, because of the deceptions, they did not expect for at least another week. Another intelligence 'black hole' concerned 21st Panzer Division, the one major armoured formation not located by Ultra or any other means, and which prevented the British taking Caen at the outset. 'Valuable confirmation that Ultra had correctly identified and located all the [other] armour in the west was provided by a [deciphered] announcement by the Inspector General of Panzer troops, Guderian, of his itinerary for a western tour on 20 April; this gave a splendid insight into the distribution of the armour a month before the landings.'[2] Other Ultra information of especial importance was the news in May, both from Enigma and Fish, that enemy reinforcements were arriving in Normandy and these enabled the Allied command to adjust their plans.

The massive bombing campaign in the weeks immediately prior to the invasion which, together with local sabotage, resulted in damage or destruction of most of the land-lines in western France, forced, as it was meant to do, a good deal of vital military information on to the airwaves. This revealed shortages of manpower and shortages of fuel, and on D-Day itself (6 June) a top air force Enigma message revealed the severe nature of the fuel shortage and the rationing thus made necessary, even these arrangements being contingent upon there being no invasion. Other Ultra revelations included the effect of attacks on Luftwaffe fighter airfields; enemy command structures; the make-up of new military formations; and damage to roads, railways and bridges.

One way and another, in the period April-June, the Allied command were well served by Ultra, but also by the French resistance (now 100,000 strong) and Allied intelligence-gathering networks in western Europe. No steps were overlooked to ensure complete surprise, coastal radar being bombed or jammed in a frantic electronic 'war', and deception carried to the point of dropping parachutists made of straw. From 7 June the number of deciphered signals going out from Hut Three to commands overseas (Italy and France) rose very rapidly, reaching 120 a day (one every twelve minutes) between June and August. This was just as well as von Rundstedt's Fish link became unreadable and remained so during the first four vital months of the invasion.

The intelligence BP was now able to send the Allies in France was often of immediate operational importance. 'Production' times were occasionally down to three to four hours, although some new army keys proved stubborn. In the initial period however, BP's old 'friends at Court', or so it must have seemed, came once more to the rescue. These were the 'Flivos' – army-air force liaison officers, described earlier, given to using their breakable Luftwaffe keys. Panzergruppe West, a mobile armoured strike force intended by Rommel to split the bridgehead in two by a concentrated attack, and then finish it off altogether, was frustrated when Ultra reported the exact position of the headquarters on 10 June, and it was destroyed in a bomber attack the same day. So many staff officers were killed that Panzergruppe West could not be put together again for two weeks, during which the initiative had passed to the Allies and the chance of concentrating a great mass of armour and using it to the utmost effect had gone.

## Operation Market Garden

Many of Hut Three's signals to commands in France would comprise what is called 'order of battle' information, such as strength returns, under numbered headings, such as: Personnel; Materiel (arms, ammunition, vehicles, etc.); State of Training; Special Difficulties; Operational Readiness. Another large group of signals would relate to requests for reconnaissance, e.g. by aircraft, reports of the day's fighting, and assessments of Allied intentions. In the midst of coping with their frantic workload, the staff of Huts Six and Three would be sometimes stopped in their tracks by a message of quite momentous significance.

> No one who was in Hut Three in August can forget the incredulity and excitement which greeted a decode on the tenth which conveyed Hitler's personal order for the renewal of the Mortain offensive: for a few moments before Montgomery and Bradley received it, we could sense on our own that three German armies might be surrounded and destroyed in what came to be called the Falaise pocket.[3]

Ultra now surpassed itself, quickly giving key warnings of enemy intentions, enemy confusion, and making possible swift and decisive Allied action. As Bennett points out, aerial reconnaissance might show what the enemy were doing at a certain moment, but only Ultra could show what he intended to do an hour or two later. By September the Allies had become not just confident, but overconfident; there was even official speculation that the Germans might have given up by 1 December, and this may have led to a decline in the influence of Ultra. Such confidence, however, was soon to be rudely shaken. In the prevailing euphoria the disastrous Arnhem airborne operation (Market Garden) was planned, and evidence from both Ultra and photographic reconnaissance was tragically ignored. 'Even Ultra's strong indications that two or more Panzer divisions were quartered on or near the Market Garden battlefield could not penetrate the wall, "cemented by confidence, complacency and an uncharacteristic refusal to weigh evidence", which some of its recipients had erected to protect their presuppositions.'[4] Lower echelon intelligence officers who, unaware of Ultra, raised doubts about the wisdom of the operation, attracted a good deal of 'flak'.

## Ultra and the Ardennes offensive

The unsuccessful assassination plot against Hitler in July made him more distrustful of his generals – those that there were left – than ever, and even more determined to intervene in military operations. On 4 September the British had captured the port of Antwerp which Hitler saw as a significant threat if it became a major supply port. Meanwhile, partly as a result of the Arnhem failure, the enemy were preventing the Allies making full use of the port by their control of the surrounding areas, and militarily there was a situation of stalemate. Hitler himself had planned an offensive in the Ardennes as far back as August. Three army groups comprising twenty-five divisions were assembled under Field Marshal Model of which the Sixth Panzer Army was newly set up under the trusted Nazi, SS General Dietrich. Having found the weakest part of the Allied front, the plan was to reach the Meuse in one mighty bound, and thereafter Brussels, Antwerp and the sea. It was a crackpot idea, grandiose in conception but thoroughly unworkable through sheer lack of resources. It was a last attempt to do something before the Allies arrived on German soil, an attempt borne of desperation. Naturally, the two men who would be responsible, von Rundstedt and Model, opposed it strenuously, and tried to convince Hitler of a more limited objective: first take Aachen, then if quick and successful, attempt Antwerp, but he would have none of it. Hitler rightly assumed that the Allies would not dream that he would attempt a rerun, in a bad winter, of the success he had achieved in the summer of 1940. Exceptional secrecy was maintained; it was the end of October before Hitler briefed the commanders, and even then in an insulting, backhanded way, by briefing their two Chiefs of Staff – accompanied by threats – presumably because he would brook no opposition and wished to avoid a confrontation. The details were prepared by Hitler's own staff, the High Command, which, as Model pointed out, had never planned a campaign before! But more and more people had to be told; it was much too big an operation to keep quiet, and the personnel and supply problems, given all Germany's other problems, were very considerable. Nevertheless, despite the weight of evidence accumulating in the two months before the battle, Allied intelligence remained, it now seems, wilfully blind.

When this attack, the last German major offensive of the War, came on 16 December, it administered a very unpleasant shock to the Allied command and especially their intelligence staffs, who had expected no such thing and indeed, had pronounced the enemy incapable of any such attack.

After the War, complaints in several memoirs by distinguished officers in the 1960s implied, because Ultra could not be mentioned directly, that Bletchley gave no warning of the attack.

Authors like Ralph Bennett and Peter Calvocoressi, both mentioned previously as senior members of Hut Three, have said that if Allied intelligence was taken by surprise, Hut Three certainly was not. 'Ultra intelligence, which was copious from start to finish of the campaign of 1944–5, gave numerous indications of a substantial offensive in the offing and in the general area of the Ardennes.'[5] The creation of the Sixth SS Panzer Army was explicitly mentioned in a BP signal of 18 September, the reinforcement of the Luftwaffe was duly reported – the force in that sector being quadrupled in size – units being transferred from as far away as the eastern front – entirely contrary to a recent edict that the main function of fighter aircraft henceforth was to be the protection of German home territory. (Intensive Allied bombing in the autumn had put thirty-five per cent of German industry out of action.) All this was highly suspicious. Bletchley also broke railway ciphers which disclosed men and materials moving in that direction.

Through his book, *Ultra in the West*, Ralph Bennett is in a strong position to rebut these allegations. The book is based on signals sent from Hut Three at Bletchley Park to commands overseas in 1944–5, all of which are open to view in the Public Record Office, and gives an absorbing account of these military operations in the autumn of 1944, seen through the eyes of the enemy whose messages were being deciphered, and also through those of Hut Three. Bennett points out that the offensive, like the Allied invasion on D-Day, was kept very secret, and also had its deception plan, '*Wacht am Rhein*' (watch on the Rhine), which carefully suggested a defensive build-up to protect the industry of the Ruhr, and which, astonishingly, seems to have been 'bought' by Allied 'intelligence' staff, although as Bennett says, the 'watch on the Rhine' cover-name was never mentioned in any Ultra signal, and one can only wonder what dubious sources were being given credence. Bennett shows, with many illustrations, that there was ample evidence for Allied intelligence to put together a picture of a major operation pending.

In addition to the Ultra evidence, Peter Calvocoressi, the Head of the Hut Three Air Section, recalls,

> some time before the offensive, one of my colleagues on the signals side . . . told me that his section had identified two new wireless networks to the east

of the Ardennes. From their configuration . . . they belonged to full-blown armies. Their corps and divisions could be counted with a fair degree of certitude and located by direction-finding. They had plainly been told to keep wireless silence which was in itself a significant piece of intelligence.[6]

He goes on to say (as we have mentioned earlier) that the wireless networks could not maintain complete silence as the controlling station needed to ensure that its satellite stations were in working order and not suffering from frequency drift. Thus there was something to intercept if not to decipher, and what it gave the listeners was 'a picture of a large ground force in a definable area and apparently holding its breath before embarking on something special'.[7] This is one of those few occasions mentioned in Appendix 4 (Bletchley in danger) when traffic analysis ranked in importance with deciphering, but alas, like Hinsley's warning to the Admiralty of the potential threat to HMS *Glorious*, it appears to have been ignored.

During this stalemate period the Allied command were so engrossed with ending the War, and so fixed on how best to reach the Rhine, that they could not imagine that even Hitler would make a dash for the Meuse. So ingrained was this attitude that some sixty miles of the Ardennes front were manned by only four divisions, two of them 'green' troops, and two recovering from previous operations.

For all the largely self-induced surprise, Hitler's gamble did not succeed, the offensive essentially failing after four days. On 22 December, von Rundstedt asked Hitler for permission to retreat, which was of course, refused, but to no avail. The campaign was marked by a very stout defence of Bastogne by American forces which detained as many as nine German divisions and generally blunted the offensive.

In these desperate closing stages of the War Hut Six deciphered from time to time, messages which might otherwise have gone out by teleprinter. On 16 September 1944, an order from the C-in-C, von Rundstedt,

emphasised that the fight on German soil must increase German fanaticism. Every pillbox, block of houses or village to be defended until allies bled to death or garrison dead... only task to hold positions or be annihilated. Commanders to ensure that this fanaticism continually increased in troops and civilians . . . Anyone, officer or man, apathetic and unaware of decisive responsibility of the hour and who did not carry out task with complete disregard for his life to be removed and proceedings taken . . .

All authorities to ensure, by comprehensive and draconian methods, that the will to resist in the troops was re-established and maintained.[8]

And towards the end of October, 'OKW (High Command) noted that further signs of disintegration had appeared and ordered the severest measures, including the immediate execution of officers in front of their own men, against anyone endangering the Wehrmacht's will to fight, while Hitler virtually imprisoned his troops on the western front by re-iterating Himmler's former prohibition against crossing the Rhine from west to east.'[9]

Thus historians who write about 'the outstanding feature of the last phase of the war' being the 'tenacity with which the Germans maintained their resistance on all fronts' in tones of semi-admiration, fail to understand the nature of the Nazi regime, which was one of terror, violence or the threat of violence, never far from the surface. In the light of the foregoing and the many former German soldiers who recall only too well having guns both in front and behind them; and hopeless positions, from which units would normally withdraw, being frequently defended to the death, one may see the regime for what it was, and why so many millions were so glad to be liberated from it.

## Notes

1. This division, so close to a landing beach, might have been spotted by photographic reconnaissance, but such were the intricacies of the cat and mouse game, with frequent switching of roles, that the Allies may have avoided too much tell-tale air activity in an invasion area.
2. Bennett, *Ultra in the West*, p. 58.
3. Ralph Bennett in Hinsley and Stripp, *Codebreakers*, pp. 39–40.
4. Bennett, *Ultra in the West*, p. 145.
5. Calvocoressi, et al. *Total War, The Causes and Courses of the Second World War* Vol. I: The Western Hemisphere (London, Penguin Books 1989) p. 550.
6. Calvocoressi, *Top Secret Ultra*, p. 47.
7. Ibid.
8. Ibid., p. 99.
9. Bennett, *Ultra in the West*, p. 171.

# TAILPIECE

The first question that occurs to most people about the wartime Enigma is this: how did it happen that an aggressive power like Nazi Germany, priding itself on its military efficiency, should have its codes and ciphers broken and read on an enormous scale in the Second World War?

In the end it may come down to what attitude is taken to making war, the offensive powers putting insufficient effort into code-making, the defensive ones concentrating on code-breaking.

After the betrayal of Czechoslovakia in 1938, and the destruction of its system of alliances with France and the Soviet Union, Hitler's Reich stood poised, dominating the European scene, able to strike in any direction without much fear of serious opposition. As a result of the phenomenal expansion of the war machine from 1935 – the Nazis having no plans for the peaceful recovery of Germany after the Depression – the country, whose main natural resources were coal and water, was plunged, by 1938, into a financial crisis. Having gained as much as possible by threats, war was then seen as the answer to the crisis. In the sudden, unprovoked, undeclared war on Poland, the world saw blitzkrieg in action. This is the lightning war, the war of rapid movement and overwhelming force applied without warning, needing, as was pointed out at the outset, speedy, reliable communication, in which, above all, secrecy can be guaranteed. Here, the Enigma system was seen as ideal for its purpose: the direction of military operations at army, corps and divisional level. In terms of blitzkrieg, code-making would be uppermost in the military mind; code-breaking associated with a long war – a war of attrition – which the First World War had so clearly shown, was beyond Germany's

162

means and which they had vowed never to get involved in again.

It is probable that in the 1930s a totally unbreakable machine cipher system, for large-scale military use, was not possible, but the designers of the Enigma machine had been far too pleased with themselves, contemplating the astronomical number of possible plugboard cross-connections (over 150 million million) and the theoretical 900 million years it might take an enemy code-breaker to work through all the permutations, to bother to examine its weaknesses, especially the necessary operating procedures, i.e. not only as a machine, but as a system.

But the faults in the machine itself might have been foreseen. To summarize those already mentioned: the fact that a letter can never 'go to itself' ('A' can never be enciphered as 'A') was a great help in deciphering; the addition of the plugboard, of which the designers were so proud, did not alter the reciprocal nature of the machine (if 'A' becomes 'G', then 'G' becomes 'A'), and could partly be ignored in deciphering; the keyboard had been connected to the entry wheel in the simplest order possible, an astonishing oversight, whereas random orders would have produced an immense number of possibilities, and may well have prevented the Poles from ever getting started.

The faults of the machine notwithstanding, Welchman maintains that 'the real culprits were the people who laid down the operating procedures, the people who were communicating with each other, and the cipher clerks who were operating the machines. The machine as it was would have been impregnable if it had been used properly.'[1]

Welchman catalogues no fewer than twelve serious errors in procedure, and suggests that careful monitoring (and correction) of seven of these, 'would have stopped us cold'.[2] For example, the endless search for cribs was greatly assisted by the very stereotyped pattern of many enemy routine orders and reports which always included not only the time of origin in the preamble to the message, but the full 'style, title and description' of both addressee and originator, long-winded enough to provide cribs in themselves. If all this meticulous Prussian correctness had simply been buried in the text, or, as Welchman suggests, 'if message generation procedures had called for the use of coded addresses and signatures, we would have been sunk.'[3] Again, when messages were being relayed, they were often retransmitted using a different key but without changing the text, giving the successful breaker of the first key a useful crib to the second. We discussed earlier the lazy habits of a few Enigma operators which provided Hut Six with 'Sillies', but it was the extremely fortunate discovery of the 'Herivel tip' that enabled hut Six to exploit these errors at the crucial moment in May 1940, when the enemy at last corrected the biggest blunder of all, the double encipherment of the indicator letters, and the entire British operation hung in the balance.

Welchman suggests that 'perhaps the most spectacular single error was the failure to think of the principles of our bombes which made an Enigma key vulnerable to a sufficiently long crib.'[4] On the other hand the bombes would not have worked without cribs, and could the enemy ever have believed that his procedures were so flawed as to provide them? But the cardinal error, Welchman insists, was the failure to monitor their own procedures which would quickly have revealed mistakes and weaknesses. Indeed, 'At any time during the war, enforcement of a few minor security measures could have defeated us completely.'[5]

One of the most remarkable, and certainly the most flagrant of errors, not untinged with humour, even endearment, at the human frailty involved, is described by Welchman. Production of the monthly Enigma key sheets was a job for some German back-room boy ('Oscar'), whose life – behind the lines – was not too hard until in 1942, with the expansion of the War, came a big increase in the number of keys. For each day of the month, as we know, he had to produce a wheel order (three out of five), three ring settings, cross pluggings and four three-letter discriminants. When four or five of these monthly sheets had increased to ten or twelve, Oscar had a bright idea. Of course he had kept copies of all the sheets he had ever issued, because they must never, never, be duplicated, but to save time and trouble, especially when under pressure, what if he took say, a ring-setting from one back sheet, a wheel order from another, and so on. It was very wrong, but life was getting a bit too hectic, and perhaps they had removed his assistant (to the Russian front?). Anyway, who would know? Well, Reg Parker of Hut Six knew straight away. He had been checking for any possible repeats at the beginning of each month for some time, looking for just such an aberration, and now, any elements of a new key that had been broken by Hut Six before, would not have to be broken again. So life became a little easier, both for Oscar and for Hut Six. Astonishing that it could happen at all, and perhaps even more astonishing that someone should be on the lookout. As Welchman said, 'Someone in Hut Six had thought of everything'. Naturally, they called it 'Parkerismus'.

164

There were six or seven German cipher bureaux which could and should have tackled these errors. But they failed to do so, and one may conjecture that they were probably at loggerheads with each other – a fate which might have overtaken BP had it not got off the ground so early and then escaped the clutches of Military Intelligence. Then, all except one, the bureaux may have become disheartened by lack of success, and finally, they or their superiors, may not have wished to face the consequences of discovering serious flaws in the Enigma system. Anyway, they might have reasoned, would it matter that much? The blitzkrieg would ensure that all would be over quickly, and indeed it might have been, if Hitler's ambitions had not been unlimited. '*Und Morgen die ganze Welt*' they sang, – 'and tomorrow the whole world'. In any case, a measure of 'damage limitation' as we would now say, was built into the system. In the worst case, if some 'effete' Briton or 'decadent' Frenchman managed to capture a monthly code sheet, its loss would soon be realized and the keys changed (as they were in North Africa in November 1941). At the very worst, the enemy would be able to decipher only for the remainder of that month's sheet, after which he would be in the dark once more, the Germans comfortingly believed.[6] Anyway, their enemy would surely be in rapid retreat, so any knowledge gained would be of little use (and this happened during the retreat to Dunkirk in 1940).

One cipher bureau was very successful. The *B-Dienst*, whose masters the Kriegsmarine and especially U-boat Command, took a very different attitude to the War and like the British they were defensive and cautious. In order to exercise tight daily control over its fleet, U-boat Command was prepared to abandon the ideal of wireless silence, or even of minimal use. Not only did the Command make extensive use of wireless but the boats themselves were required to report frequently. The risk thereby entailed of some of the many signals being intercepted and perhaps even deciphered, was considered worthwhile in order to operate the wolfpack system. To minimize this risk stringent procedures were adopted both in relation to the enciphering and transmission of messages and precautions in cases of emergency. As we have seen, messages were often doubly enciphered (officer only), first coded and then enciphered (Short Signal Book) – the latter with transmissions of extremely short duration. For emergencies there was the cue-word system, and machine-settings, for example, were printed in soluble ink on water-soluble paper. The very greatest attention was paid to the security of their signals and there were but two shortcomings, one theoretical, one practical, to which we shall return.

For all their precautions there were times, and this applies to both sides, when action taken by their enemies could only have arisen from prior knowledge of their secrets, and this knowledge almost certainly obtained from code-breaking.

When the *Bismarck*'s widely-scattered supply ships and tankers were all rashly polished off by the Royal Navy in a very short space of time, it was extremely hard to imagine that it could have come about except through code-breaking, yet the exhaustive investigation undertaken by Admiral Fricke, Chief of the Naval War Command, after taking the case of each ship in turn and analysing the circumstances of its sinking (as far as they knew), finally exonerated the Enigma system. Nevertheless, the result bears a hint of quiet diplomacy. The investigation cleared the Enigma because any other conclusion would be unthinkable in naval and political terms. The War would not stand still while an entirely new naval cipher system were developed, manufactured and installed in ships, and men trained anew. And who would tell the emperor he has no clothes – that his closest secrets had been laid bare to the enemy?

As mentioned earlier, the German naval signals authorities considered that even three out of four of the main components of the Enigma system could be captured and the enemy still remain in the dark. But why not consider the ultimate scenario – that all components might be compromised on just one disastrous occasion. Perhaps they did, even if there is no official record to that effect. As usual, actions speak louder than words.

Far from being a response to the sinking of *Bismarck*'s supply ships, or the difficulty of finding convoys in the autumn of 1941, as has been suggested, the four-wheel Enigma machine took a whole year to design, manufacture, distribute and install in the ocean-going U-boats before it came into service in February 1942 – i.e. dating back to a period before BP had even begun to decipher the naval Enigma. The measures that were taken in the autumn of 1941, the rather clumsy attempt to disguise the naval grid which indicated a U-boat's position at sea, and the introduction of the new Trident key, may be seen as temporary expedients pending the arrival of the four-wheel Enigma. The 'Address Book' method of disguising the position of U-boats (from 1 December 1941), however, was much more sophisticated, and gave BP and OIC an enormous headache, often delaying deciphering which could be complete in all but that one vital particular.

The new four-wheel machine disabled Bletchley for the rest of 1942, that very bad year at sea, and would have continued to do so, but for a mighty enemy blunder. After the very lucky capture of U-559 Hut Eight were able to work out that the new machine was still largely being used, in effect, to simulate the old three-wheel machine (although, e.g. sending weather reports, for which this was necessary, was but a minor part of the traffic). This was an enormous relief to Hut Eight, as they were able to manage without the use of four-wheel Bombes, which they neither had, nor had they the prospect of acquiring any. I have seen no explanation of why the great advantage of the four-wheel machine was thrown away, but if any reader, perhaps a German, could enlighten me, I should be grateful.

The other failure, of a theoretical nature, was not to consider the risk entailed in recipherments – when the same or a very similar message, e.g. storm or mine-laying reports, is sent out in more than one cipher, say, in Dockyard and an Enigma key – success in deciphering one giving a possible entry into the other. But this arises, as Welchman said, from the enemy failure to consider the principle of the Bombe, which depends on the cribs that recipherments produce. These recipherments became the basis of much of Hut Eight's work.

But the Germans were not alone in all this. The British Admiral who complained that the first he knew of the position of enemy forces was when one or more of his ships was sunk, suggests the Admiralty were forgetting the lessons of the First World War when British code-breaking had allowed the Royal Navy to anticipate the movements of the enemy fleet. However, in August 1940, the Naval Code and Cipher were both given new editions. In 1942 the Admiralty stoutly repelled the notion that their signals were being read by pointing to Operation Torch, which achieved complete surprise, although the elaborate Allied deception plan played an important part in this. But again, their deeds belie their words. In December 1942, as the Battle of the Atlantic was being lost, the Admiralty took a defensive measure to counter possible deciphering; and enciphering the indicators actually threw B-Dienst into turmoil for two whole months during which the disastrous rate of sinking suddenly lessened – in itself an astonishing piece of evidence. And there is no doubt that the Admiralty and the relevant section of BP were agonisingly slow to implement the new cipher – two years of trials at a leisurely peacetime pace while ships and men were going to the bottom.

On the other hand, the German Navy's meticulous concern with the security of its signals could be carried too far. Too much security can be self-defeating. For example, printing lists of Enigma settings in water-soluble ink (and on soluble paper), although easy to destroy deliberately by dousing in case of emergency (or if sunk in coastal waters where enemy divers could find them), means also that they are just as liable to destruction by the accidental toppling of a bottle of beer. A spare set must therefore be kept, preferably under lock and key. The initial discovery of a list of machine settings in the wreck of the *Krebs* during the Lofoten raid in 1941 was of just such a spare set in a sealed envelope in a locked drawer of the captain's cabin, forced open by the British boarding party.

This was BP's first significant break into the German naval Enigma, and was the result of just a little too much security.

## Notes

1. Welchman, *The Hut Six Story*, p. 168.
2. Ibid., p. 167.
3. Ibid.
4. Ibid., p. 164.
5. Ibid.
6. Even if in possession of a code sheet an enemy would still have to determine that randomly chosen text setting.

# Appendix 1

# THE CODEWHEEL

Towards the end of the First World War four men residing in the Netherlands, Germany, Sweden and the United States, independently of each other, had developed the principle of the codewheel. These small wheels, made of an insulating material such as Bakelite, had a series of brass contacts spaced around the circumference of the wheel on both sides. The twenty-six contacts, one for each letter of the alphabet, were connected by wires to the contacts on the other face of the wheel in random order. If we call one side the input contacts, and the other side the output contacts, an electric current fed to the input contact for, say, the letter B, may turn out to be connected to the output contact on the other side for, say, the letter K. It will all depend on the way the wheel has been wired. The wiring is the secret of the codewheel, and code-breakers try hard to work out the wiring of enemy codewheels. If, in the above example, the letter B were part of a word in plain language (not coded), like 'blue', the letter K, its output contact, could be said to be enciphered, and might form part of an enciphered word or complete message.

Imagine that each of the input contacts on the codewheel is connected to a typewriter-style keyboard, and that each of the output contacts is connected to a lamp, which will light up a letter of the alphabet. Pressing one of the typewriter-style keys will send an electric current (supplied by a battery) through both input and output contacts and light up one of the lamps. For example, if pressing key B lights up lamp K, and pressing key L lights up lamp J, U lights up G, and E lights up O, the word 'blue' would have been enciphered as 'kjgo'. The problem here is if the cipher machine had only one codewheel B would always change

169

into K and it would not remain secret. The object of the designers of these machines was to make the number of possibilities of turning one letter into another as great as possible. Adding a second or a third code-wheel would add complexity, but without other changes it would not defeat the code-breakers for long.

In the machine invented by Scherbius in Germany the codewheel was able to revolve. It was placed between two fixed plates or drums, each with a set of contacts on one face only, and these came into contact with the adjacent face of the moveable codewheel (with its contacts on both faces)[1] and then, each time the typewriter key was pressed, the wheel moved one place (from one letter contact to the next), being one twenty-sixth of a complete revolution. This results in the route taken by the electric current on its journey from key to lamp being varied each time the key is pressed. If we have a word with a double letter, for example, 'seen', the two 'e's' would be enciphered differently, and might become, say, 'nb'. A wheel with twenty-six letters which revolves twenty-six times, would give a possible total of 676 different routes that the current could taken between keys and lamps before returning to the original route.[2] The German Enigma machine, as it was eventually called, had, in its military version, three revolving wheels, giving $26 \times 26 \times 26$ i.e. 17576 possibilities. The wiring of wheels 2 and 3 was different from wheel No. 1 and from each other. The wheels were geared together, much like those of an adding machine, so that after twenty-six moves of the right-hand wheel the centre wheel was actuated by a notch cut in the wheel ring and moved one space. When the centre wheel itself reached its 'turnover position' it actuated the left-hand wheel to move one space – this latter revolving very slowly. The wheels would thus be in constantly varying positions in relation to each other providing new circuits from key to lamp.

Early in 1918 Scherbius had offered the German Navy his machine, pointing out that even if an enemy were in possession of the machine, the key (i.e. the wheel starting positions known only to sender and receiver), could not be found, and the message could not be deciphered, without going through (for an eight-wheel machine) some six billion starting positions. Nevertheless, the Navy, blind to their own failings, turned it down, while acknowledging its good security.

The commercial machine, now called Enigma, was publicized by Scherbius and his Cipher Machine Co. at the International Postal Union Congresses in 1923–4, but they had little success selling it to banks and business firms. Some time in 1924, however, the German Navy, though small, began to take an interest. They had belatedly realized that the British had been reading their coded signal intelligence for a good part of the First World War, probably when they read, to their chagrin, war memoirs like those of Winston Churchill, which gleefully pointed up British decoding successes and their benefit to naval operations.

Meanwhile, the Enigma machine had made progress. A smaller, more compact, four-wheel model had been developed with lamps lighting up letters in place of a complicated printing attachment, and usually referred to as the 'Glow Lamp' model. Several improvements included wheels which could be removed from the machine and replaced in a different order; a ring displaying the letters of the alphabet which could be turned independently around the wheels themselves, and could be fixed in a given position so that the 'ring position' given in the key would not be the same as the position of the wheel itself, adding a further layer of security.[3] Four – eventually three – removable wheels made the machine much more practicable for shipboard or field use, as opposed to the eight-wheeled monster that Scherbius had first built. The fourth wheel was turned into a fixed reversing plate (*Umkehrwalze*) so that the current which had taken a particular route through the machine was now sent back by a different route before lighting its lamp. The reversing plate had the usual twenty-six contacts, but only on one side. This doubling of the current's route through the wheels had an important effect. If pressing key B lit up lamp Z, then pressing key Z would now light up lamp B. This new reciprocal character of the machine eliminated the need to switch from enciphering to deciphering position or mode, thus preventing an operator under stress trying to encipher while the machine was still in deciphering mode. Conversely, the reciprocal feature proved helpful to the decipherers, especially as the new arrangement also meant that a letter could not represent itself; keying E would never result in an E, and this proved a serious weakness.

The naval version of this machine went into service in 1926 with strict procedural and security safeguards which we shall mention later. After two years the Army followed suit with simpler procedures perhaps better adapted to military campaigning. In 1930 the German Army modified the machine in an important way with the introduction of a plugboard (*Steckerbrett*) on the front of the machine with twenty-six pairs of sockets into which plugs or jacks on the ends of twin leads could

171

be inserted rather like a small telephone switchboard, the sockets being marked in the usual German keyboard (QWERTZU) fashion. These additional connections, made each time the machine was set up, had the effect of vastly increasing the number of possibilities of enciphering letters. The army experts were no doubt extremely pleased with themselves, especially as, at least in theory, the foreign code-breaker might now be faced with having to make a billion attempts to solve one enciphered message! Another cause for satisfaction was that the effect was much as if the machine had been redesigned with an additional number of wheels, thus avoiding the complication and cost entailed. The addition of the plugboard was the big change, and the one that distinguished the military from the commercial version of the Enigma machine. But it did not affect the reciprocal character of the machine and the weakness that no letter could be enciphered to itself. Nevertheless, the Germans believed they had brought the machine to the point where it could not be 'broken'. Their ingenuity however, did not extend to the procedures for actually using the machine, and this enabled the Poles to mount a successful attack, and only two years later.

At the outbreak of war the naval version of the machine had an additional three wheels to choose from, each with two turnover notches (3 out of 8) giving 336 possible wheel orders, as compared with the Army's 3 out of 5, and a possible 60 wheel orders.

Electrically, the plugboard was interposed between the keyboard contacts and the wheels, thus again altering the route of the current (in fact altering it twice owing to the action of the reversing drum both before entering the wheels and after coming from them.) This resulted in two additional 'swappings' of letters so that with only six or seven pairs of letters connected – as was the army practice in the early 1930s – the number of states the machine might be in could be several billion! The keyboard comprised twenty-six letters and no numerals. These would have to be spelled out.

## Notes

1. To ensure a good electrical connection, the contacts on the right side were spring-loaded, those on the left side flat.
2. This figure assumes no repeated letters.
3. This removed the fixed correspondence between the motion of the wheels and their internal setting.

# Appendix 2

# OPERATING THE ENIGMA MACHINE (MILITARY AND AIR FORCE) FROM 15 SEPTEMBER 1938 UNTIL MAY 1940

There would usually be a team of three: two Enigma operators or cipher clerks (No. 1 and No. 2) and a wireless operator. First of all the No. 1 would set up the machine in accordance with printed instructions. The monthly key sheet, with a set of operating instructions for each day, had five columns:

1. Date (at 00.01 hours).
2. Wheel order (*Walzenlage*) This column would specify three numbered wheels (out of five), e.g. V II III, inserting them in the machine in that order.
3. Ring setting or position (*Ringstellung*) The clerk would adjust an independently-rotatable alphabet ring – instructions given in figures, e.g. 01 07 12 = AGL – starting with the wheel on the left.
4. He would connect (from 1.1.39) ten pairs of plugs (twenty letters), e.g. GF KV JM etc. (i.e. G connected to F, etc.).

The fifth column headed '*Kenngruppen*' was not a part of the key, and was included in the preamble shown below.

The following would be transmitted by the wireless operator as the unenciphered (plain language) preamble to the message.
There were six items:

1. Call-sign (changed daily), e.g. G5Z to KGG and 4QK.
2. Time of origin, e.g. 17:15.
3. Number of letters in message. There was a minimum of fifty letters sent in groups of five letters and a maximum of 250. Long messages were sent in parts, each part enciphered separately, with its own indicator setting, text setting and indicator.
4. Whether message was a complete single message, or formed part of a two-, three- or four-part message.
5. *Kenngruppen*, e.g. azs, one out of four three-letter groups printed under the fifth column of the daily instruction sheet. These distinguished or 'discriminated' between the keys issued to various types of traffic (army, SS, police, etc.), preceded by two 'filler' letters, e.g. x or y.
6. The 'indicator' setting; a randomly chosen three-letter group, e.g. JEF. This was to indicate to the receiving clerk (i.e. if he had the key (No. 5)) to set his wheels in this way.

As mentioned in item 6 of the preamble (above), the cipher clerk had already chosen a three-letter group, entirely at random, the 'indicator setting', and turned his wheels accordingly. ('random' meant no abbreviations or initials, e.g. of girlfriends or repeats (XXX) or short German words (ist))

He then chose a further three letters at random, say JCB (the 'text setting') and (with the wheels set at JEF) keyed it twice over, JCBJCB which might be enciphered by the machine as say, BQROMP (the six-letter 'indicator'), the No. 2 clerk noting it down letter by letter.

The 'indicator' now became the first six letters of the enciphered message, and would include the first five-letter group plus the first letter of the second group.

Lastly, the clerk would turn his wheels to JCB, the 'text setting' and tap out the text (usually in German) letter by letter, the No. 2 clerk taking down the enciphered version from the lamps and passing it to the wireless operator for transmission in Morse, the text or message proper, beginning with the second letter of the second five-letter group.

The receiving clerk, assuming he had been issued with the key, would already have his machine set up in exactly the same way. As the machine was designed to be reciprocal, there was no need to switch to 'deciphering mode' nor would there be any undue delay. The preamble would have given him his 'indicator setting' so he would have set his wheels to JEF. The very first six letters of the enciphered message being the 'indicator', he would key BQROMP and obtain JCBJCB (if the two triplets differed, e.g. due to transmission difficulties, he would ask for it to be sent again.) He would then set his wheels to JCB and decipher the message proper, keying it letter by letter, his No. 2 recovering the message or 'text' from the lamps.

From May 1940, at the time of the invasion of Western Europe, the second triplet ceased to be used. The random choice of text setting, JCBJCB, was keyed once only, JCB, which would have produced BQR in place of BQROMP. (From May, both the indicator setting, JEF, and the indicator BQR, would be included in the preamble by the clerk sending the message.) Doubling the text setting had at last been seen as a weakness; in fact it was a monumental blunder on the part of the Germans, and had enabled first the Poles and then the British to break into the 'invulnerable' Enigma system.

# Appendix 3

# SETTING UP THE NAVAL
# ENIGMA MACHINE

First of all, an officer would have to select and set the wheels (three out of eight) and rings every other day according to a machine-settings or key list (the 'inner settings').

The Enigma operator then continued, step by step, to follow a long, complicated procedure ('outer settings' changed daily). He would refer to the machine-settings list for a basic or ground setting (*Grundstellung*), to which his wheels were turned, and he would also insert the plugs as instructed.

He would then choose a three-letter group, say HYU – the message indicator – by referring to an indicators book (*Kennbuch*). When tapped out on the machine this trigraph would produce the message setting – the three letters which would appear in the apertures or windows – of the machine when finally he reached the point when he could actually send the message. Meanwhile, he took those first three letters chosen from the indicators book, and combined them – by filling in squares in a worksheet – with a second set of three, also chosen at random from the indicators book, say VFN.

They would appear in the 'Bookgroup' column of the worksheet staggered as follows:

        H Y U
      V F N

He would then invent filler letters to fill the vacant squares, say X and L.

Next, he would encipher the first vertical pair by looking up the letters XV in a secret bigram table, and replacing them with the cipher pair, which he would enter on the sheet, repeat the process for the other three pairs, and would end up with two, now enciphered, four-letter groups, say,

I LAT
B S H U

He now tapped out the message indicator (as above) and entered at the top of his message form the three letters which lit up, and rotated his wheels until these three message-key letters showed in the windows.

He finally transmitted ILAT BHSU, followed by the enciphered message. The receiving operator would not have the problem of possible errors in the indicators – which originally caused the military, very mistakenly, to doubly-encipher them, as the bigram tables were recip-rocal, and the receiving operator knew that if XV became IB in that bigram table, then IB would become XV. Having deciphered the in-dicators the receiving operator would have recovered the message key or setting, and would be able to decipher the rest of the message.

With this system, tedious but secure, little was left to chance. Unlike the military Enigma where the operator was required to invent indicator settings himself, with the risk of repeated initials of girlfriends, etc., these indicators were not only chosen from a book and then crossed out, not to be used again, but were enciphered using the current bigram table as specified in the daily machine-settings list. There were nine or ten of these tables valid for a lengthy period.

Further details of the naval procedure, with facsimiles showing parts of a worksheet, indicators book, bigram table and distribution list (denoting which columns of the indicators book were relevant to the key in use, e.g. Home Waters key) are to be found in Kahn, *Seizing the Enigma*, pp. 285–90.

# Appendix 4

# BLETCHLEY IN DANGER

In September 1941, the Director of Military Intelligence made a second and more determined effort to gain control of BP from the Secret Service. The main burden of his argument was that the War Office was putting increasing resources into interception stations and traffic analysis but it had not seen much return in terms of hard intelligence. The fact that the Luftwaffe had made extensive use of the Enigma whereas the German army had not, and so results were mainly of interest to the RAF (although a lot of military intelligence had come via the army/airforce liaison officers), was hardly Bletchley's fault; nor were delays caused by acute shortages of personnel and equipment. But the DMI was making a case. His traffic analysis group, under MI8, had been slogging away at German army and air force wireless networks and call signs for eighteen months, and had finally cracked the system of allocation of call signs. This was important in that it provided some real military intelligence as they now often knew which enemy units were which, and, with the aid of direction-finding, if they were lucky, where they were. It was also of help to BP in deciding on daily priorities in tackling the various keys. But it was not to be compared with deciphering, and apart from a few occasions during the War when all else failed, traffic analysis played only a limited role. The army section at BP regarded it as a 'a fad', although Welchman and others maintained it often helped with cribs, recipherments and even with independent intelligence. But this success strengthened the military's hand and they wished to transfer their Traffic Analysis Section, now grown to over one hundred strong, to Bletchley Park, which scared Denniston (Head of BP) for several reasons. As the military provided two elements, interception and traffic analysis, they objected to BP controlling the actual work of the interception stations, although as Welchman had so ably demonstrated, interception and code-breaking were inseparable, and control of the stations was fundamental to BP's work.

The MI8 colonel was a strong advocate of all signal intelligence in time of war being under military control. It was alleged that the sigint programme was suffering from lack of effective operational control and that whatever the official arrangements, 'actual control, such as it was, was being exercised by GC&CS and thus by people "who rightly have no touch with the Operational and Planning Directorates of the Ministries, and no knowledge of our future operations".'[1] One would never imagine from the superior aggrieved tone that the record of military intelligence up to the autumn of 1941 had been anything but disastrous! Here, however, was a new, successful, mixed service and civilian, rapidly-growing organization (approaching 1,500 people), but under civilian administrative control, and rather loose, inadequate control at that. As they would say nowadays, 'ripe for a take-over'. Unfortunately for the DMI, the other two Directors of Intelligence did not support him in his demand for the reorganization of signal intelligence. This was because they were reasonably satisfied with the existing arrangements, and in any case, probably preferred Bletchley's discreet guidance to control by the military. The situation was exacerbated when army and air force intelligence officers were seconded to Hut Three in 1941, and although now attached to the Secret Service they remained loyal to their old service. They were soon in conflict with Hut Three's 'old guard' who had developed intelligence techniques enabling them to evaluate and service most messages, allowing recipients the benefit of important additional or background information which the 'raw' decode would not reveal. The new officers regarded such 'servicing' as 'interference' in military matters, and worse, implied a distrust of the service intelligence directorates. Asserting that they understood the needs of the 'client' departments far better than any civilians could, some of these officers took control over parts of Hut Three, and one can only conjecture that they had been sent to disrupt rather than assist, and prepare the way for a military takeover.

In the manner of military intelligence the world over these officers were probably expert in departmental in-fighting, and may have exercised their skills accordingly. Edward Thomas, one of the Official

History team, comments, 'Certain fairly senior, but very able, service officers (regulars) took advantage of complaints from Whitehall at the turn of 1941/2 to bid for control of certain sectors of [BP's] now immensely influential output. Those at the coal-face sensed the tension.'[2]

The actual situation, no doubt very distasteful to these officers and their superiors, was that Hut Three, in particular, had turned itself into a far more efficient intelligence organization than its Whitehall counterparts. The funny academics, in their tweeds and pullovers, had shown that they could understand certain military matters very well, and knew far more about the enemy fighting forces than Whitehall did. With their ever-growing indexes, research facilities, technical experts, specialized 'back-room' groups – staffed by clever, hard-working, people – Hut Three had become an intelligence organization the like of which had never been seen, or even imagined, in the antiquated, stuffy, military establishment. As for service and civilian staff working side by side, although subject to different codes of discipline, things had worked smoothly enough until the recent arrivals from MI. In order to ease the situation, the head of SIS made a concession by transferring operational control of the 'appreciation' sections (3A and 3M) to the senior air and military officers at BP. But this only led to friction between these senior officers who promptly fell out with each other as well as with Denniston (Head of BP). Things got worse and by January 1942 when 'the spate of argument and recrimination was damaging efficiency and threatening a breakdown of discipline',[3] Menzies (Head of SIS) appointed an independent investigator to enquire, not only into the matters under dispute, but into the entire administrative control of GC&CS which had clearly outgrown the capacity of both the original structure and its personnel.

The Official History does not disclose the terms of reference under which the investigation was conducted, but one cannot help recalling that, most fortuitously, the four leading boffins had sent their letter to Churchill as recently as October 1941 which had resulted in 'action this day', and that 'C' (Menzies) did have access to the Prime Minister, and anyway the results speak for themselves. The enquiry was concluded by the end of January, the recommendations being that as far as the management of BP was concerned, Commander Denniston and his immediate staff were transferred to London, there to carry on the diplomatic and commercial code-breaking activities – now a small sideshow – with the former deputy head at BP, Commander Travis, becoming undisputed Head (subject only to 'C'), a move clearly hinted at in the boffins' letter. Travis was given a new strong organization, and individual heads of sections, even though many were civilians, were given complete control of their service personnel. Hut Three and its output was placed under a strong administrator, Wing Commander Eric Jones (later, as Sir Eric Jones, Director of GCHQ), who promptly restored tranquillity and efficiency – the Hut retaining and indeed, strengthening, its intelligence activities, and its relations with the Whitehall directorates improving enormously.

Once again, luck, as well as common sense, was on Bletchley's side – but it was another 'close-run thing'. The essence of Bletchley's success, as the years following the February 1942 reorganization were to show, was in its very centralization, its all-inclusiveness. If parts had been hived off by the military, we would have seen an inevitable return to divided authority, crossed lines, bickering and confusion. There were still some 'secret shows' engaged for better or worse, in signal intelligence, but all the key intelligence-gathering functions were 'under one roof' at BP, or were carefully controlled or co-ordinated from there. This gave the advantages necessary for decoding and intelligence processing on an industrial scale (in August 1944 signals to commands overseas were leaving BP at the rate of one every twelve minutes) and making a real contribution to winning the War.

## Notes

1. Official History, Vol. II, p. 23.
2. Hinsley and Stripp, *Codebreakers*, p. 45.
3. Official History, Vol. II, p. 26.

# Appendix 5

# ENIGMA AND
# SZ 40/42 (TUNNY)

There are similarities between these two systems, but they are largely superficial. The Enigma is a letter-swapping cipher machine with three interchangeable wheels and cross-pluggings able to produce a vast number of states which, in theory, the machine could be in at any one time. It did not print out its messages which had to be taken down letter by letter from the lamps before being passed, e.g. to a wireless operator, distinctly, as the jargon has it, 'off-line'. True, both machines could encipher and decipher, but whereas the Enigma was the size of a large typewriter, portable and designed for robust field conditions, the *Schlüsselzusatz* SZ40/42 was sizeable and intended for static operation. The Enigma was set up each day, with a few simple operations which could be done quickly. It had two design weaknesses which, coupled with procedural and human error, rendered it liable to successful attack from an enemy. It was not used above Army HQ level.

The SZ40/42, the German military (not air force) machine, used for communication at the very highest level, was a standard Lorenz teleprinter with a cipher 'attachment' – but not a small one. First the machine turned its messages, which had been tapped out on the keyboard, into the usual teleprinter pattern (or 'code') and then enciphered them – through the twelve-wheel 'attachment', before transmitting them via a land-line to a similar machine at the other end, which would decipher the message before turning it back from teleprinter 'code' into plain language and finally printing out the message. This is an automatic, on-line, non-Morse, high-speed, transmission – unless the message has to be sent over the airwaves, in which case a wireless transmitter and receiver were required. Like the Enigma, the cipher machine had to be set up in advance, but the operations were more complicated and much more time consuming.

To decipher Enigma messages in large numbers, an electro-mechanical machine, the Bombe, was used as an analytical tool to try and reduce the very large number of possibilities of solving the key down to a small manageable number, and even doing it right first time. This required a 'crib', an accurate estimate of what some part of the original message contained (although at this stage the message was still enciphered in 'gobbledygook'), and a 'menu' – instructions for setting up the Bombe. If the crib were correctly placed and the cipher letters used in the menu correctly received, it would deliver settings (nothing else), and an Enigma set up accordingly would decipher into plain language. With comparatively few 'links' established for the top-level Fish traffic, the cipher machine with its twelve wheels seemingly offering astronomical[1] numbers of permutations for enciphering, the German authorities obviously assumed the system was one-hundred-and-one per cent watertight before allowing messages to be sent by wireless. But it was not. Three processes were necessary before the enciphered messages could be unscrambled and the plaintext recovered.

First, the very difficult task of discovering the tooth patterns of the wheels ('wheel breaking').[2] Next, the individual wheel settings for each transmission had to be found ('wheel setting'). Lastly, having (miraculously) derived the setting-up instructions, it was necessary to have similar – or similarly functioning – machines to those of the enemy so that they could be set up in exactly the same way as the originator of the message, and so decipher successfully.

The first of these processes was carried out in the 'Testery' by 'hand methods', for which we have no detail, but generally include both mathematical and linguistic attacks – if only from the presence of high-powered mathematical and wordy people. The second was eventually aided by Colossus, in the 'Newmanry'; the last by BP's own very secretly-built 'Tunny' machines. These were not copies of the original SZ40s (we are told that no machines or drawings were ever captured) but cleverly simulated to perform the same functions as German SZ machines.

As explained on pages 148–9 the builders of the simulated Tunny machine very ingeniously used standard telephone engineering components in place of wheels. The American team under William F. Friedman, struggling in 1939-40 to break the Japanese Type 97 Alphabetical Typewriter (code-named 'Purple'), eventually discovered that the machine used stepping switches from the dial telephones of the day in place of wheels!

## Notes

1. The mathematical period of all twelve wheels of the Tunny machine (SZ 40/42) was about $1.6 \times 10^{19}$(!)
2. Unlike Enigma, the facility for changing wheel-tooth patterns meant that the wheels themselves did not need to be changed, although twelve was quite enough.

# BIBLIOGRAPHY

There is now a considerable body of literature about code-breaking and about Bletchley Park. Some of it is specialized, covering particular aspects of the subject, and may be technical or mathematical.

A short list of books, well-researched or written from first-hand expert knowledge, would include the following:

Bennett, Ralph, *Ultra in the West: The Normandy Campaign of 1944–45* (London, Hutchinson, 1979).

Bennett, Ralph, *Ultra and Mediterranean Strategy, 1941–45* (London, Hamish Hamilton, 1989).

Calvocoressi, Peter, *Top Secret Ultra* (London, Cassell, 1980).

Hinsley, F.H., et al, *British Intelligence in the Second World War*, vols. I–V (London, HMSO, 1979–90), The Official History.

Hinsley F.H., and Stripp, Alan (eds), *Codebreakers: The Inside Story of Bletchley Park* (Oxford, OUP, 1993).

Hodges, Andrew, *Alan Turing:The Enigma* (London, Vintage, 1992).

Kahn, David, *Seizing the Enigma* (London, Souvenir Press, 1992).

Welchman, Gordon, *The Hut Six Story* (Cleobury Mortimer, Baldwin, 1997).

Books in which code-breaking plays an important part:

Beevor, Antony, *Crete – The Battle and the Resistance* (London, John Murray (Publishers) Ltd.).

Masterman, J.C., *The Double-Cross System* (London, Pimlico, 1995).

A good general history of the War which includes material on Ultra intelligence:

Calvocoressi, Peter, Wint, Guy and Pritchard, John, *Total War, The Causes and Courses of the Second World War*, Vol. I: *The Western Hemisphere* (London, Penguin Books, 1989).

For more detailed reference:

*The Oxford Companion to the Second World War* (Oxford, OUP, 1995).

For a day-to-day, week-by-week, account of the War:

Gilbert, Martin, *Second World War* (London, George Weidenfeld and Nicholson, 1989).

# INDEX